Autobiography: A Very Short Introduction

VERY SHORT INTRODUCTIONS are for anyone wanting a stimulating and accessible way into a new subject. They are written by experts, and have been translated into more than 45 different languages.

The series began in 1995, and now covers a wide variety of topics in every discipline. The VSI library currently contains over 550 volumes—a Very Short Introduction to everything from Psychology and Philosophy of Science to American History and Relativity—and continues to grow in every subject area.

Very Short Introductions available now:

Available soon:

For more information visit our website

www.oup.com/vsi/

Laura Marcus

AUTOBIOGRAPHY

A Very Short Introduction

OXFORD
UNIVERSITY PRESS

Great Clarendon Street, Oxford, OX2 6DP,
United Kingdom

Oxford University Press is a department of the University of Oxford.
It furthers the University's objective of excellence in research, scholarship,
and education by publishing worldwide. Oxford is a registered trade mark of
Oxford University Press in the UK and in certain other countries

First edition published in 2018

Impression: 1

Published in the United States of America by Oxford University Press
198 Madison Avenue, New York, NY 10016, United States of America

British Library Cataloguing in Publication Data
Data available

Library of Congress Control Number: 2018937072

ISBN 978-0-19-966924-0

Printed in Great Britain by
Ashford Colour Press Ltd, Gosport, Hampshire

*In memory of Micky Sheringham,
from whom I learned so much.*

Contents

Acknowledgements

My thanks to the team at Oxford University Press, in particular Andrea Keegan and Jenny Nugee. The Oxford Centre for Life-Writing, founded by Hermione Lee at Wolfson College, has been a constant source of intellectual and creative stimulation during the writing of this book. I am, above all, deeply grateful to William Outhwaite for his help in bringing it into being.

Acknowledgements

List of illustrations

Introduction

Autobiography continues to be one of the most popular forms of writing, produced by authors from across the social and professional spectrum. It is also central to the work of literary critics, philosophers, historians, and psychologists, who have found in autobiographies not only an understanding of the ways in which lives have been lived but the most fundamental accounts of what it means to be a self in the world.

The term 'autobiography' (coined at the close of the 18th century) breaks down into its component parts—'auto' (self), 'bios' (life), 'graphein' (writing). The element of writing or text is inscribed in the term itself. Language, as well as the workings of memory, shapes the past. The neologism autobiography has been followed by a succession of new terms—'autography', 'autothanatography', 'autobiografiction', 'autofiction'—as if to express the hybrid and shape-changing qualities of a genre which sets out to represent the complexities of human life, experience, and memory.

In recent years, 'life-writing' has become a widely used term in literary and cultural studies. Life-writing, and the related category 'personal writing', covers a broad range of texts, including autobiography, biography, letters, memoirs, and diaries. The emphasis is placed on the ways in which such literatures represent the lives of individuals, whether those of another or others, as in biography/group biography, or of the self, as in autobiography, journal, or diary. The use of personal writing as a term points to the fact that writing need not have made its mark in the public sphere, or have achieved publication and wide dissemination, to count as 'literature'. This has opened the way for the study, in particular, of a range of women's writings from earlier periods and for a recognition of the significance of 'personal' or 'private' writing, including family memoirs, diaries, and journals.

While the category of life-writing suggests a broad and inclusive approach to the study of literature and culture which we might associate with our contemporary moment, it was in fact deployed in the 18th century, alongside 'biography', whose usage can be dated from the 17th century. Prior to the use of autobiography as a term, critics and commentators might refer to 'self-biography' or 'the biography of a man written by himself'. This suggests that it was still perceived as unusual in secular contexts for a writer to turn his or her regard inward, though this was the guiding principle of many earlier spiritual and religious texts.

Not all autobiographers are writers by profession, though there is a widespread assumption that the literary writer's autobiography best defines the genre, and that the particularities of the life-story may be less interesting than the ways in which they are remembered and recounted. The literary writer's autobiography also bears on, and frequently comments upon, his or her other works. Such texts, and in particular those from the 19th century onwards, will often recount the ways in which a writer entered into the profession or 'vocation' of literature. The life thus becomes identified as a 'literary life'.

More broadly, autobiographical writing is seen to act as a window onto concepts of self, identity, and subjectivity, and into the ways in which these are themselves determined by time and circumstance. Autobiographies have also provided historians, in particular social historians, with crucial 'first-person accounts' of events and movements, and of the ways in which individual lives were lived at particular historical and political junctures. While, as I have suggested, autobiography is frequently defined primarily as a literary genre, it in fact exists on the borderlines between many fields of knowledge.

Autobiography as a genre became of central significance to literary theory, as it emerged in the latter decades of the 20th century. The critic Philippe Lejeune, whose work on life-writing has been highly influential in recent decades, defined autobiography as 'a retrospective prose narrative produced by a real person concerning his own existence, focusing on his individual life, in particular on the development of his personality'. This immediately raises problems of exclusion: there is no obvious reason why autobiography can only be composed in prose, and though there are few autobiographical narratives written in poetic form, William Wordsworth's autobiographical poem *The Prelude* is central to any history of autobiographical writing. Beyond this, however, Lejeune's central concern was with the question of 'identity' in autobiographical writing, and with the 'pact' that is set up between text and reader, whereby the latter can be assured that the author's name designates a real person and that the narrator and the protagonist are one and the same.

The value of Lejeune's approach lay in its attention to the textual aspects and generic markers of autobiography. He wrote extensively, for example, about the various uses of first-, second-, or third-person narrative in autobiographical writings, and of the ways in which these different forms represent the writing self's relationship to the past and present self, or selves, which it depicts. Lejeune's concept of 'the autobiographical pact' also focused, in significant ways, on the relationship between the author, the text, and the reader as the guarantor of autobiographical authenticity. It provided a flexible model of the genre and an understanding of the historical and institutional contexts in which a given work will be received and read as autobiographical.

Lejeune's vocabulary of 'pact' and 'contract' has, however, been criticized for its 'legalism'. For the literary theorist Paul de Man, the attempt to define autobiography was a fruitless endeavour: 'autobiography...is not a genre or a mode, but a figure of reading or of understanding that occurs, to some degree, in all texts'. The drive to define and demarcate autobiographical writing is thus countered by an equally strong sense that autobiography escapes final definition. For one thing, any narrative of the self and its life-story will entail a reconstruction, subject to the vagaries of memory, which renders the division between autobiography and fiction far from absolute.

Most writers and readers would, however, probably agree that works of autobiography lay claims to truth which are different from the constructed realities of fiction. Autobiography exists in a realm in which truth and falsehood are meaningful terms. Few people would apply these terms to fictional works, though we might find characters or situations unconvincing or at odds with our experience of the world. Yet autobiography also asks of its readers that they be open to the complexities of truth. These include the work of memory and the gaps produced by forgetting; the distinction between experience revived (as if, for example, from the child's point of view) and recalled (from the perspectives of an adult narrator); the conception of the self from the 'inside' and from the 'outside', as reflected back to us by others. 'Properly speaking', the psychologist and philosopher William James wrote, 'a man has as many social selves as there are individuals who recognize him and carry an image of him in their mind'.

Numerous writers of autobiography, from across the centuries, have offered their own understandings of the motives for autobiography, its possible forms, and its intended readerships. Prefaces, or opening statements, frequently anticipate the charges of vanity, egotism, self-distortion (or self-promotion), and narcissism that might be levelled against the author who talks about him or herself, answering them in advance by suggesting more edifying or altruistic autobiographical motives. Some writers of autobiography will suggest that they are on a quest for self-understanding, while others will stress their wish to communicate their experiences to others. On occasion, the writer will seek to redefine the autobiographical act itself, as in the case of Gandhi. Responding to the words of a friend who had told him (inaccurately) that 'writing an autobiography is a practice peculiar to the West', Gandhi writes in his Introduction to the book published as *An Autobiography*: 'it is not my purpose to attempt a real autobiography. I simply want to tell the story of my numerous experiments with truth.'

The individual's life and life-story may be unique, but its value will often be said to lie in its representative or exemplary status. The 19th-century philosopher John Stuart Mill opens his *Autobiography* (1873) with the assertion that 'I do not for a moment imagine that any part of what I have to relate, can be interesting to the public as a narrative, or as being connected with myself'. It rather offers, he continues, the record of an 'unusual and remarkable' education while, 'in an age of transition in opinions, there may be somewhat both of interest and of benefit in noting the successive phases of any mind which was always pressing forward, equally ready to learn and to unlearn from its own thoughts or from those of others'.

The political economist and author Harriet Martineau began to write her autobiography when she believed herself to be close to death (she in fact lived for another three decades). 'From my youth upwards', she states in her Introduction, written in 1855, 'I have felt that it was one of the duties of my life to write my autobiography'. 'A strong consciousness and a clear memory of my early feelings' equipped her for a task that seemed more pressing as her life became 'a somewhat remarkable one'. Here the autobiographical motive is defined as 'duty', though Martineau was, and is, by no means alone in turning to autobiography as a way of forestalling would-be biographers (in a growing culture of celebrity) and claiming the right to tell her story in her own terms.

Charles Darwin's *Autobiography*, written in 1876 and published posthumously in 1892, is presented, like Mill's, as 'an account of my mind and character', attempted not only for his own amusement, but because it 'might possibly interest my children or their children'. The great natural scientist and theorist of evolution thus envisages a record of interest to his descendants, while he has attempted 'to write the following account of myself, as if I were a dead man in another world looking back at my own life'. His words point up not only the important connections between 'biology' ('life-knowledge') and 'biography' ('life-writing') but also one of the essential paradoxes of the autobiographical genre: that the record of a fully completed life could only be written by 'a dead man'.

Many autobiographers have found strategies—formal and experiential—to deal with the fact that the life-stories which they recount are of necessity incomplete. Moreover, the self continues to be an evolving, changing entity, moving in the flux of time, even as the autobiographer seeks to capture and compose it. We tend to think of autobiographies as single, once-in-a-lifetime endeavours, but there are in fact numerous examples of serial autobiographies, as well as those composed and revised over many years.

The rise of the memoir in recent decades—in status and popularity—could in part be understood as a response to the problems of representing a 'whole' life. In the 19th and early 20th centuries, the distinction (at least in English-language contexts) was often drawn, or implied, between autobiography as a sustained and serious self-investigation and memoir as a more outward-facing record of experiences and events. In our own times, the evaluative distinction between those who are capable of introspection, and hence of 'proper' autobiography, and those 'memoirists' who are not, has largely been lost, and there has been a marked rise among authors in the use of the term 'memoir' or 'memoirs'.

This need not, however, lead us to the conclusion that 'memoir' (understood as the narration of a particular set of experiences and encounters, or of a specific aspect of the self) has replaced 'autobiography' (understood as the attempt to write a life in full, or at least in the fullness of a particular life-stage, such as childhood or early years). 'Autobiography' continues to be used as a generic marker and in book titles. At the same time, there is considerable interchange between understandings of what constitutes 'autobiography' and what 'memoir'. Celebrity autobiography is now frequently written (or 'ghosted') at an early stage in the author's life. In professions, such as sport or the entertainment industry, where the career may be relatively brief, the standpoint from which past and present are observed will often lie not towards the end of the life but at the time of its flourishing.

The rise of 'memoir' may indeed be more telling as an indicator of the contemporary attractions of 'truth to life' and the representations of lived experience (defined by one critic as 'reality hunger') than of the weakening of 'autobiography' as a significant literary and historical form. The autobiography/ memoir distinction seems to have become less absolute than it was in previous centuries, and will not be used as a shaping principle in this study, though neither will the terms be used interchangeably.

The American novelist William Gass has written:

> There are differences between diaries, journals, and notebooks, just as there are differences between chronicles and memoirs and travels and testimonies, between half-a-life and slice-of-life and whole-loaf lives, and these differences should be observed, not in order to be docile to genres, to limit types, or to anally oppose any mixing of forms...but in order that the mind may keep itself clean of confusion.

7

This introduction to autobiography also seeks to avoid confusion and to respect the differences between forms, but nonetheless to acknowledge the productive interplay between them. Many autobiographies will, for example, make extensive use of diaries and letters, written or received. In doing so, they seek to recapture a past present, an immediacy, within the retrospective form of the autobiography. Travel writing has traditionally been kept as a separate category from that of autobiography, but there are frequently significant links between the two forms of writing and record.

More complex issues, addressed in Chapter 8, arise when there is an intermingling of fact and fiction. This characterized the genre of the novel as it flourished in the 18th century, at a time in which (as in the writings of Daniel Defoe) the novel would frequently be represented as the personal record of its hero or heroine. Such intermixing has returned as a central feature of modernist and contemporary writing, as in the *roman à clef* and autobiographical fictions of novelists such as D. H. Lawrence and James Joyce, and in the rise of autofiction in the present day. In exploring such developments, this study will acknowledge the often porous relationships between fiction and autobiography, while continuing to affirm the distinctive properties of autobiography as a practice of writing and as a representation of experience.

Chapter 1
Confession, conversion, testimony

While autobiography can certainly be defined as a literary form, it reaches into, and overlaps with, many other kinds of writing and fields of knowledge. This is particularly clear in the case of the models—confession, conversion, testimony—discussed in this chapter, which bring the literary into relation with concepts central to religion, law, and history. These models also bear on questions that have been fundamental to understandings of autobiography: truth, authenticity, selfhood, narrative time, memory, the relationship between past and present selves, the motives for writing an autobiography, and the identities, imagined or real, of the autobiography's addressees or readers.

Confession and autobiography are linked in significant ways. Two of the most influential writers in the autobiographical tradition—St Augustine and Jean-Jacques Rousseau—make 'Confessions' their title. Conversion and the 'turning point' are often central to the narrative structures both of confession and of autobiography. The writing 'I' seeks a stable position from which to look back on the past as it moves towards the present, and to imagine a future, though this is often combined with the Augustinian model of a split and doubled self: the old and the new. In many secular autobiographies, the conversion moment of spiritual texts emerges as an epiphany or a life-crisis and, more generally, in the relationship between, as Virginia Woolf put it in her autobiographical work 'Sketch of the Past', 'I now, I then'.

Confessions

The term 'confession' relates to the different, though at times overlapping spheres of the religious, the legal, and the literary. For the intellectual historian Michel Foucault, we have become 'confessing animals', and there is an argument that the proliferation and popularity of autobiography and memoir (which are part of a continuum including the 'true confessions' genres of popular culture) in modern times are part of this confessional turn. In the 20th century, psychoanalysis (and psychotherapy more generally), which is based on the remedial nature of the dialogue between analyst and patient, could also be said to be shaped by confessional models.

Complex issues arise over the nature of confession as interrogation (a demand for confession from an external authority) and as voluntary, arising from the will of the confessing subject. Confession produced under compulsion must cast considerable doubt on the 'truth' that has been extracted. Yet, as the literary and legal theorist Peter Brooks has argued, religion and law have a centuries-long commitment to confessional processes and practices. Autobiography is the modern form of writing emerging out of the long history of confessional discourse: confession is, in Brooks's phrase, 'a fragment of autobiography'.

St Augustine's *Confessions* (written in the 4th century) has marked, for the Western literary tradition, a point of origin for autobiography and established a dominant structure for confessional and conversion narratives. Augustine recounts the story of his childhood and youth, dwelling on his sinful condition, before the scene of revelation in a garden. Cast down by his knowledge of himself as a sinner, the despairing Augustine hears a voice which repeats the refrain 'Take it and read, take it and read' ('Tolle lege'). He opens his book of Scripture and reads a passage exhorting men to 'arm yourselves with the Lord Jesus Christ'. '[I]n an instant', Augustine writes, 'it was as though the light of confidence flooded into my heart and all the darkness of doubt was dispelled'. Augustine locates—as would the centuries of autobiographers following him—the turning point (or points) in his life. This (or these) can, of course, only be recognized retrospectively, becoming part of the autobiographical narration rather than of experience itself.

The final sections of the *Confessions* move into a 'timeless' meditation on Augustine's relationship to God. He addresses his words throughout the *Confessions* to an Omniscient God, who knows his story and his 'inmost thoughts', but Augustine is also mindful of his earthly readers as he makes his confessions 'both in my heart before you [God] and in this book before the many who will read it'. The *Confessions*, written before any tradition of private writing existed, contains elements that would become central to later introspective and autobiographical literature, including the question of who is to be the reader or recipient of the text. Augustine presents his 'inner self', in his 'sinful' state, as a 'house divided against itself', and agonizes over the question of why the mind cannot order itself as can the body. He meditates on questions of time, eternity, and memory, invoking what we might now call the 'unconscious' in his reflections on the paradox that memory, 'a vast, immeasurable sanctuary', is not contained in the mind: 'Although it is part of my nature, I cannot understand all that I am'.

He explores the division between inner feeling and outer show, as in his response to the death of his beloved mother, and the question of sincerity and truth in autobiography. How, he asks, are those other men who hear him speak about himself to know 'whether I am telling the truth, since no one *knows a man's thoughts, except the man's own spirit that is within him*?' He addresses questions of self-knowledge and self-consciousness: 'Oh Lord,

I am working hard in this field, and the field of my labours is my own self. I have become a problem to myself [*Mihi quaestio factus sum*]…I am investigating myself, my memory, my mind.' 'I have become a problem [or "question"] to myself': the words echo throughout the nearly two millennia of introspective and autobiographical works that followed the *Confessions*. The issue of how the self can know itself, central to philosophical and psychological enquiry, is addressed more fully in the following chapters.

Spiritual autobiography and conversion narratives

In *The Life of Saint Teresa of Ávila by Herself*, St Teresa records her path to conversion, which took place in 1555. Her reading of St Augustine's *Confessions* is depicted as a fundamental event and, like Augustine's 'Tolle lege', as a turning point in her life: 'I seemed to see myself there […] When I came to the story of his conversion, and read how he heard the voice in the garden, it seemed exactly as if the Lord were speaking to me.' There is a transmission from one autobiographical narrative to another, across the centuries. This is shown in the powerful identification with another self and, in the case of the spiritual and mystical texts which recount a relationship with Christ, with the body and its suffering. Works such as the 14th-century anchoress Julian of Norwich's *Revelations of Divine Love* have been defined as 'incarnational autobiography', with self-knowledge seen as deriving from knowledge of Christ's body, and word and flesh becoming one.

The Book of Margery Kempe, transcribed in the 1430s, has been claimed as the first English-language autobiography, though it was written by more than one amanuensis or scribe and its subject is referred to throughout in the third person, and as 'this creature'. The early chapters give an account of Margery Kempe's worldly engagements, which she renounces in order to dedicate herself to the religious life, including celibacy (after she had given birth to some fourteen children). The opening 'proem' (preface) provides an account of the motives for the writing. The task of justifying the act of autobiography and, in particular, of forestalling any charge of 'vanity' or 'narcissism' attached to writing about the self, is an aspect of the genre that has remained remarkably consistent to the present day. The Proem asserts that many clerics begged Kempe to let them write the story of her religious experiences, but she refused consent until some twenty years later, when 'our Lord . . . commanded her and charged her to have her feelings and revelations and her way of living written down, so that His goodness might be known to the whole world'. The demand to produce an account of the self is thus represented as coming from the highest authority.

While Augustine's *Confessions* (addressed to God) contain no acts of confession to an earthly interlocutor, Kempe's book speaks of her frequent acts of confession. The relationship between the religious rituals of confession and the autobiographical work as a confessional form emerges strongly in the 'Puritan' confession. Lacking the formal (and private) sacrament of confession and penance, Protestant Christians took up the idea of a narrative of the self, while requiring that it also be backed up by a record of virtuous deeds. Whether or not, like the earliest Protestants, they had explicitly experienced a conversion, the image became dominant; one of the earliest memoirists, James Fraser of Brea in Scotland (1639–99), wrote that 'A Man's whole Life is but a Conversion'.

John Bunyan, whose *Pilgrim's Progress* (1678) has been described as the first English-language novel, earlier wrote a prison memoir, *Grace Abounding* (1666), in which Bunyan does not describe a *single* episode of conversion, but rather a gradual progress like that of his pilgrim protagonist. His autobiography is motivated partly by his imprisonment in 1661, after the restoration of the monarchy and the Anglican church, for illegal puritan preaching. As well as the enforced separation from those he calls his 'children',

he was driven also by the sense that he needed to record his
spiritual travails.

The 19th-century theologian John Henry Newman converted
from Anglicanism to Roman Catholicism, having earlier believed
and preached that the pope was Antichrist. He came gradually to
feel that the separation of England from the universal (Western)
church had been both a misfortune and a mistake, and he embraced
without difficulty Catholic doctrines such as transubstantiation
and papal infallibility. The Preface to his autobiographical work
Apologia Pro Vita Sua (1864) records the familiar concern that
he should 'come to write a whole book about myself, and about
my innermost thoughts and feelings', but over 200 pages later
he records his 'perfect peace and contentment' since his
conversion in 1845. The narration of the life-story—'this history
of myself'—concludes at this point, though the final chapter
continues, following the model set by Augustine's *Confessions*,
with meditations on matters of religious faith and creed.

Romantic confessions

The Romantic writers and thinkers of the 18th and early
19th centuries played a central part in the formation of modern
understandings of selfhood and, relatedly, modern autobiography.
The 'confessional' mode returns, this time in secular as well as
spiritual contexts, though throughout the 18th and 19th centuries
God continues to be invoked as the final and ultimate auditor and
judge of autobiographical accounts of a life.

Jean-Jacques Rousseau's posthumously published *Confessions*
(divided, like Augustine's, into twelve sections or 'books' and, like
many autobiographies, a composite work written and rewritten
over many years) was a highly influential work, although Rousseau
insists in the opening paragraph that he is engaged in an enterprise
'which has no precedent, and which, once complete, will have no

imitator. I want to display to my kind a man portrayed in every way true to nature, and this man will be myself.' Rousseau claims the representation of his unique selfhood as the justification for the autobiography, and promises the absolute truthfulness of his account: 'I have displayed myself as I was'.

The substance of his 'confessions', as they relate to his early years, bears on a lie and a betrayal; 'shame' is a keynote of the text, as it is throughout the long histories of spiritual and secular autobiographies. Until the point of writing, Rousseau claims, 'I have never been able to take the step of relieving my heart by confessing this to a friend', and the motivation for writing the *Confessions* has in part arisen from his desire to rid himself of 'the terrible deed' (the youthful theft of a ribbon and the laying of blame on a young woman servant) on his conscience. This is autobiography as exculpation. Rousseau, like the Romantic writer and autobiographer Thomas De Quincey and the late 19th-century Irish poet and novelist George Moore (author of *Confessions of a Young Man* (1889)), is haunted by memories of a lost figure: a young, poor, and vulnerable female companion. She seems to represent a second self, whose fate or fading is the condition for the survival of the authorial self, though her loss, or abandonment, is permanently coloured by guilt and regret.

Rousseau's emphasis on the formative nature of childhood experience marks a new emphasis in the history of autobiography. It is an aspect of the question as to whether the self is created by 'nature' or 'nurture'. This was at the heart of Rousseau's philosophical writings, as of his period more broadly, and has remained a perennially significant topic, in whose exploration autobiographies have been seen as a central resource. Rousseau represents his early childhood as a period of, for the most part, innocence and happiness, which is then irrevocably tainted by injustice and cruelty. He also dwells on the early formation of sexual desires—those which we would now term 'masochistic' and which Rousseau represents as abnormal—through a 'childhood punishment' which 'would determine my tastes, my desires, my passions, my self for the rest of my life'.

The more bitter and paranoid later sections have a very different quality to the first books, in which Rousseau, writing from the perspective of age, expresses his delight in the recall and recounting of his early memories: 'It is as if, feeling my life escaping from me, I were trying to recapture it at its beginnings'. Here it is the author's 'pleasure' in recovering his past which is said to drive the autobiography, rather than the confessional and self-justificatory modes which dominate elsewhere in the text, and Rousseau makes a plea for the reader's indulgence rather than appealing to his or her powers of judgement.

The motives for autobiographical writing are thus seen to be multiple, mirroring the complexities of the represented self. Rousseau refers frequently to his 'characteristic contradictions': for him, as for Augustine, the self is a 'problem' or 'question' to itself. Autobiographies may indeed tell the stories of lives, and of the events that compose them, but they are also texts engaged with fundamental issues of selfhood, personality, character, and identity. They are, moreover, invariably written from the perspectives of a present looking back at the past, and the ways in which that past is remembered may be more significant than the absolute truth (even if such a thing were recoverable) of the events themselves.

The question of fact and fiction in autobiography (whose differentiation from the novel must depend upon some notion of veracity or authenticity) is a difficult and contested one. For Rousseau, as for the Romantics more generally, there is a concept of 'truth' which is legitimated less by 'fact' than by 'feeling', a distinction also suggested by the critic George Henry Lewes in his 1847 review of Currer Bell's (Charlotte Brontë's) novel *Jane Eyre*: 'It is an autobiography,—not, perhaps, in the naked facts and circumstances, but in the actual suffering and experience' (see Figure 1).

JANE EYRE:

An Autobiography.

BY

CURRER BELL.

IN THREE VOLUMES.

VOL. I.

THIRD EDITION.

LONDON:

SMITH, ELDER AND CO., CORNHILL.

1848.

1. First edition title page of *Jane Eyre*.

Rousseau profoundly shaped the literary and philosophical traditions in which writers of the Romantic period and beyond would take their own selves as a subject. For this, he received praise and blame in varying measures throughout the 19th century. The English Romantic writer Thomas De Quincey's best-known work, *Confessions of an English Opium-Eater*, opens with an attack on that French literature (for which one can read Rousseau) which offers 'the spectacle of a human being obtruding on our notice his moral ulcers or scars'. This example, De Quincey suggests, made him hesitate before offering up his own 'act of confession' to the public eye, and he does so only 'in consideration of the service which I may thereby render to the whole class of opium-eaters'. He thus claims a moral imperative (offering himself up as an object lesson) which, he implies, is lacking in the self-display of Rousseau and his kind.

De Quincey's *Confessions* and, to an even greater extent, its companion text *Suspiria de Profundis* describe at length the dreams and delusions he experienced under the influence of opium. The realms of the imagination become a central dimension of experience, in a reworking of the visionary consciousness explored by earlier spiritual and mystical writers. In the Preface to *Confessions*, De Quincey argues that his dreams are of value to the extent that he is a philosopher, with 'an inner eye and power of intuition for the vision and the mysteries of our human nature'. If 'the power of dreaming' is said to be the faculty most at risk in a frenetic, politically volatile, and industrializing modern society, one of the most significant roles for the autobiographer must be to focus on an inner landscape. The world of his dreams is, moreover, a repetition of 'the experiences of childhood'. Here we see De Quincey offering an understanding of mental life which anticipates some of the central tenets of Freudian psychoanalysis, including the nature of memory and the mind as a 'palimpsest' (defined by De Quincey as 'a membrane or roll cleansed of its manuscript by reiterated successions', but bearing the traces of earlier inscriptions). There is, De Quincey writes, 'no such thing as *forgetting* possible to the mind'.

We should also note here the significance of metaphors of printing/imprinting as ways of imaging memory and, relatedly, autobiography as life-writing. One of the earliest American autobiographers, the 18th-century writer and politician Benjamin Franklin, began his career as a printer and compositor. Throughout his autobiography, he describes mistakes in his life as 'errata', as if his life were a script marked by printing errors, as well as their subsequent corrections, and as if the history of his experiences were a kind of 'inventory' (see Figure 2). We cannot actually live our life over again, in a (preferably revised) 'second edition', but we can, using autobiography, bring it back through recollection, made durable by putting it down in writing.

The rise of modern Western autobiography is closely intertwined with developments in print culture and the creation of a broad public readership. The democratization of writing and the expansion of readership test the model of 'confession' as a private and intimate act. In the Preface to *Confessions*, De Quincey seeks to differentiate his autobiography from the so-called 'confessions' of his time (which would have included the 'gallows confessions' of convicted criminals) issuing forth from, in his words, 'demireps, adventurers, or swindlers'. Autobiography, by the time in which De Quincey was writing, had entered the realms of popular literature, creating increasing anxiety over the usurpation of 'confessional' and autobiographical literatures by subjects who were, as a result of their class, occupation, or moral bent, perceived to be unworthy or reprobate subjects. In his 'Autobiography', Franklin quotes a letter from the political economist Benjamin Vaughan, who had encouraged him to write the story of his life as a good example to others: 'it will make a point of comparison with the lives of various public cut-throats and intriguers, and with absurd monastic self-tormentors or vain literary triflers'. Its

THE

PRIVATE LIFE

OF THE LATE

BENJAMIN FRANKLIN, LL.D.

LATE MINISTER PLENIPOTENTIARY FROM THE UNITED
STATES OF AMERICA TO FRANCE, &c. &c. &c.

Originally written by Himself,
AND NOW TRANSLATED FROM THE FRENCH.

TO WHICH ARE ADDED,

SOME ACCOUNT OF HIS PUBLIC LIFE, A VARIETY OF
ANECDOTES CONCERNING HIM, BY M. M. BRISSOT,
CONDORCET, ROCHEFOUCAULT, LE ROY, &c. &c.

AND THE EULOGIUM OF M. FAUCHET,
CONSTITUTIONAL BISHOP OF THE DEPARTMENT OF CALVADOS,
AND A MEMBER OF THE NATIONAL CONVENTION.

Eripuit cœlo fulmen, mox sceptra tyrannis. TURGOT.

A Paris, ce grand homme, dans notre ancien régime, seroit resté dans l'ob-
scurité; comment employer le fils d'un chandelier ? LE ROY.

LONDON:

PRINTED FOR J. PARSONS, NO. 21, PATER-NOSTER ROW,

2. English title page of *The Autobiography of Benjamin Franklin.*

purpose would be, Vaughan suggests, to induce 'more men to spend lives fit to be written'.

De Quincey, by contrast with Franklin, does not present his life as a model one. His object was, he wrote, 'to display the marvellous agency of opium, whether for pleasure or for pain'. He does, however, invoke, however ironically, an earlier model of 'confessional' writing, as in his reference to 'the public (into whose private ear I am confidentially whispering my confessions)'. Throughout the *Confessions*, he refers to instances of 'error' (as in his fateful decision to leave school, which necessitated his earning his living as a jobbing writer) which are also turning points. The revisions to the 1821/2 text, which he carried out in 1856, reveal the extent to which he wished to revise the earlier version of his life, but the autobiography (like the life) can never be error-free.

Confession and testimony in the modern age

In his essay 'The Critic as Artist', Oscar Wilde wrote that 'Humanity will always love Rousseau for having confessed his sins, not to a priest, but to the world'. The late 19th- and early 20th-century 'religion of art' produced a number of autobiographical texts which followed, and at times parodied, spiritual autobiographical writings. They include Moore's *Confessions of a Young Man* and James Joyce's *A Portrait of the Artist as a Young Man*. In Joyce's text, religious and secular confession are intertwined.

The legacy of Rousseau's *Confessions*, in its mixture of confession and accusation, is also apparent in Wilde's own autobiographical work *De Profundis*. Published some years after Wilde's death, *De Profundis* was his last prose-work, composed in the final months of his incarceration in Reading Gaol as a punishment for 'gross indecency'. Written as a letter to his former lover, Lord Alfred Douglas, *De Profundis* is in part Wilde's fierce accusation against Douglas for the ruination of his life and his art: 'You knew what my art was to me, the great primal note by which

I had revealed, first myself to myself, and then myself to the world'. The central portion of the letter takes a different turn as, rather than addressing Douglas directly, Wilde meditates on Christ and on the self-realization that comes through suffering. In the book's final pages, Wilde returns to his address to Douglas, contemplating, at the book's end, the possibility of their meeting after Wilde's release.

In *De Profundis*, Wilde indicates the ways in which the prisoner is denied or loses those dimensions of selfhood and life which would seem essential to autobiographical narration. These include the flow of lived time ('we who live in prison...have to measure time by throbs of pain, and the record of bitter moments', Wilde writes), a name and an identity ('I myself...had no name at all', he states of his first months in prison). Yet the conditions of imprisonment have produced particularly intense and charged examples of autobiography throughout the centuries.

The political and ethical importance of confession has returned in notions of restorative justice such as the South African Truth and Reconciliation Commission in the late 1990s, a forum in which witnesses who had suffered under the regime could give evidence and the perpetrators of violence could, on the basis of their confessions, seek amnesty. '[Apartheid] set for itself the task of reforming—that is, deforming and hardening—the human heart', the South African writer J. M. Coetzee wrote in *Giving Offense*, his 1996 study of censorship, and 'if we want to understand it, we cannot ignore those passages of its testament that reach us in the heart-speech of autobiography and confession'. Coetzee has written extensively about the significance of confessional writing, historically and in the present day. The confessional texts to which he has repeatedly returned in discussion include works by Augustine, Rousseau, Tolstoy, and Dostoevsky. Throughout his work, he has pointed to the paradoxes of confession, arguing (as did the theorist Paul de Man) that the confessional act is bound to breed a desire for yet more confession: it feeds on itself and can never be satisfied. Coetzee's novel *Disgrace* suggests, moreover, that neither truth nor reconciliation is likely to arise from within formal institutions and the regulated processes of confessional speech.

Coetzee's trilogy of memoirs, *Boyhood, Youth*, and *Summertime*, presents the autobiographical and the confessional in unexpected ways. Both *Boyhood* and *Youth* are written in the third person, distancing the narrator/autobiographer from his past selves. *Boyhood* is deeply, though ironically, linked to the Rousseauian tradition of confessional autobiography. In *Youth*, 'he' moves from university in South Africa to work in London. An aspiring writer, his self-image as an artistic spirit draws strongly from Joyce's *A Portrait of the Artist as a Young Man*, which has its own intense and ironic relationship to confession, shame, and desire. *Summertime* breaks with the narrative of the growing self: the (auto)biographical subject is a dead man. A young English writer is writing a biography of the recently deceased John Coetzee and gathers material from those, in particular his women lovers, who 'knew' him in life; failures in intimacy and of knowing mark their recollections.

Boyhood, subtitled 'Scenes from Provincial Life', tells of early years in South Africa. The past is not presented as if filtered through the memories and perspectives of the adult self: there is no indication of a future. School and home enclose the self, in time and space. The feelings 'he' experiences are familiar from the confessional tradition of autobiography; throughout the text the narrator refers to shame, lies, secrets. Yet, unlike Rousseau's *Confessions* which, as Coetzee has written, combines confession and excuse in recounting the incident of the theft of the ribbon, there is no self-justification in *Boyhood*. The boy's feelings bear not only on the witnessing or the perpetrating of specific injuries—as in his crushing of his younger brother's finger in a corn-grinder ('the memory lies like a weight upon him')—but also on the shame, and the damage without end, brought about by colonization.

Testimony and trauma

Like confession, the concept of testimony brings out the relation between legal deposition and autobiography, while also pointing to a broader notion of 'bearing witness' and even of an obligation to do so. A significant number of autobiographical narratives written, or told to others for writing and editing, by African-American slaves were produced in the late 18th and the 19th centuries. Among the best known and, at the time of their publication, most influential of these are works by Olaudah Equiano, Solomon Northup (author of *Twelve Years a Slave*), Frederick Douglass, and Harriet Jacobs.

In 'Narrative of the Life of Frederick Douglass, an American Slave', Douglass (the surname he was given when he escaped from the slave-owning South to the North) recounts the story of his life from his early years, many of them spent on a slave-plantation, to his arrival in New York in 1838 as a fugitive slave. Douglass opens the autobiography, in familiar enough fashion, by naming his birthplace, but in the second sentence he states that he has 'no accurate knowledge of my age, never having seen any authentic record containing it'. Nor does he know the identity of his father, though he believes him to have been a white man, and there are rumours that he may have been his 'master'. Throughout the autobiography, Douglass points to the ways in which 'knowledge' of all kinds—of self and of the world—is withheld from and denied to slaves, and represents his acquisition of knowledge—in particular the ability to read and to write—as his 'pathway from slavery to freedom'.

Douglass's autobiography is the fruit of his self-education, against all the odds. His ability to tell and to write not only his story but also those of his fellow-slaves—victims of the utmost cruelty and violence at the hands of Southern slave-owners—makes it possible for him to 'testify' to this history. 'Testimony' was legally denied to slaves and 'colored people': they could not, in law, bring a white man to account for his actions nor testify against his word. In writing his autobiography, Douglass produces his 'testimony' and asserts his 'freedom'. As Henry Bibb, another former slave, wrote in the Preface to his autobiography: 'I also wanted to leave my humble testimony on record against this man-destroying system, to be read by succeeding generations when my body shall lie mouldering in the dust'.

Harriet Jacobs' *Incidents in the Life of a Slave Girl* (written under the name Linda Brent) ends at the point where her 'freedom' is bought, after years spent in hiding as a fugitive slave. Despite her gratitude to her benefactor, Jacobs cannot resign herself to being regarded as a 'piece of property', to be bought and sold. 'Every man has a property in his own person', the 17th-century philosopher John Locke wrote. Such self-possession, and indeed personhood, is denied the slave, who is perceived as nothing more than a chattel. The autobiography is at once an assertion of identity and personhood and, like Frederick Douglass's text, an indictment of the broader system of slavery, with a very direct address to the reader. The personal story provided crucial evidence and impetus for the abolitionist cause. The autobiography at times takes on aspects of the sentimental novel and of melodrama: this 'literary' dimension of many slave narratives has led some historians to perceive them as inauthentic historical 'evidence'. Such a judgement overlooks the ways in which autobiography can combine the historical and the literary. Jacobs used literary techniques (such as reported speech) to engage her readers, but she also insisted on the importance of factual record, copying letters and other documents into her text.

Exceptional or extreme historical circumstances, such as war, are fertile ground for the writing of the literatures of testimony and witness. The experiences undergone by both men and women during World War I resulted in a great many published memoirs and autobiographies, though for the most part their appearance was not immediate, coming a decade or more after the war's end. In writing her *Testament of Youth* in the early 1930s, Vera Brittain noted her desire to bear witness to the experiences of the women who went to war (in Brittain's case, as a Voluntary Aid Detachment nurse). Brittain is explicit about the relationship between immediacy and retrospect; she writes in her Foreword of her extensive use of 'old letters and diaries, because it seemed to me that the contemporary opinions [...] of youth in the period under review were at least as important a part of its testament as retrospective reflections heavy with knowledge'.

The role of the autobiographer as witness had particular force and significance in the case of the autobiographical texts written by those who had endured incarceration in Nazi concentration camps, among them Jean Amery, Elie Weisel, Bruno Bettelheim, and Ruth Kruger. One of the earliest, and now most prominent, of these memoirs was the Italian Jewish chemist and writer Primo Levi's *If This Is a Man*, composed a few months after he had been liberated from Auschwitz. Its sequel, *The Truce*, recounts the story of his journey back to Italy from the camps.

As Levi, along with others selected for work rather than the gas chambers, enters the camps, he becomes aware 'that our language lacks words to express this offence, the demolition of a man'. With their transformation into slaves, 'many social habits and instincts are reduced to silence'. Levi records a recurrent dream, which he discovers is a shared experience for almost all the camp-inmates: that of returning home and telling his story to family and friends, only to discover that they are indifferent and unhearing. He terms the dream 'the ever-repeated scene of the unlistened-to story'. In the 'Preface' to *If This Is a Man*, Levi wrote that: 'The need to tell our story to "the rest", to make the "rest" participate in it, had taken on for us, before our liberation and after, the character of an immediate and violent impulse'. The lesson he early learned from a fellow camp-inmate was that 'even in this place one can survive, and therefore one must want to survive, to tell the story, to bear witness'.

A more recent memoir, the historian Otto Dov Kulka's *Landscapes of the Metropolis of Death*, is a series of fragmentary recollections and images from the time which Kulka, between the ages of ten and eleven, spent in Auschwitz. The memoir opens with his return, as an adult, to the camps. As he walks through their ruins, he sees the crematoria: 'I am held captive there as a life prisoner, bound and fettered with chains that cannot be undone'. It was, of course, the condition of his survival that he was never in fact in the crematoria, though as a child 'I circled them as a moth circles a flame'. The 'Metropolis of Death' was the logic of the place and the condition of his childhood being, and it continues to return to him in his dreams. Kulka thus indirectly answers the charge that camp survivors are unable to testify to the ultimate atrocities that occurred.

Kulka includes many visual images in his text—drawings, maps, photographs—and the past (including events which he did not see with his own eyes, among them the annihilation of childhood friends and family members in the gas chambers) 'comes back in images'. Some experiences remain resistant to recall: they cannot be visualized. Whereas 19th-century narrators such as Douglass and Jacobs insisted on the absolute truth of the experiences that they recounted, and represented themselves as having near total recall of situations and conversations, the 20th-century and contemporary autobiographer is more likely to point to the gaps in memory. These are often understood as the effect of traumatic experience, and of the fluid interchange between dream, memory, and event. For Kulka, as for Levi, the world of the camps existed outside the terms of known experience and the 'truth' of the witnessing is not undermined but strengthened by the partial, fragmentary, and at times dream-like nature of its telling.

In the context of 'Holocaust denial', however, the truth of witness becomes a particularly charged and contentious question, and 'the Wilkomirski affair' has become notorious. In 1995, a Holocaust memoir by Binjamin Wilkomirski entitled *Fragmente* (*Fragments*) was published to great critical acclaim. It was presented in the form of the shards of memory emerging from the years its author had allegedly spent as a child in two concentration camps, before being smuggled out to Switzerland. The events appear through the eyes of a child who does not understand the world into which he is thrown, and the reader must fill in the gaps in the narrative.

It was subsequently discovered that *Fragments* was an invented memoir, whose author, born as Bruno Grosjean, had spent the entirety of the war years in safety in Switzerland. The historian Stefan Maechler, who has conducted extensive research into the circumstances described in the memoir and into the identity of its author, concludes: 'There is not the least doubt that Binjamin Wilkomirski is identical with Bruno Grosjean, and that the story he wrote in *Fragments* and has told elsewhere took place solely within the world of his thoughts and emotions'. Maechler does not suggest (though other commentators have) that *Fragments* was a deliberate hoax, but that its author, who has continued to insist on the truth of his account, translated memories from his own troubled early years (as a fostered child) into 'those images that society offers and accepts for the narration of horrible experiences'; in Wilkomirski's case, Nazi terror.

Wilkomirski's motivations will almost certainly remain a mystery, but the case has more general implications. The connections between the cultures of memoir and of trauma in recent decades have rendered questions of memory, truth, and representation ever more complex; trauma is now frequently understood as the aftermath and effect of a psychic injury so great that it exceeds the possibility of its 'evidentiary' narration. Yet the Wilkomirski case also suggests that referential truth continues to be judged as an essential element in autobiography in its role as the literature of witness.

Chapter 2
The journeying self

There is a close connection between the rise of autobiography in the late 18th and early 19th century and the growing fascination with travel for its own sake, or for the sake of self-development, and walking as a valued activity rather than just a necessity. With the rise of European Romanticism, Rousseau's celebration of walking, Goethe's Italian Journey, his fiction of Wilhelm Meister's *Wanderjahre*, and his autobiography, and Wordsworth 'wandering' in the Lake District initiate a pattern of links between life-writing and travel which continued through the American 'road trip' and more recent 'urban walking' (including the movement known as 'psychogeography') and the literature of landscape. Often the narrative will present a virtual or real return to places experienced earlier in the writer's life, with the usual ambivalence accompanying nostalgia. Can or should one 'go back'? Was the remembered time lost, in the sense of gone for ever, or wasted, *temps perdu*? This was also the age which saw the birth of the Bildungsroman, the 'novel of formation', or 'novel of education', which typically traces the youthful development of an individual, and the shaping of his (or, less usually, her) mind and character, as he/she moves towards maturity and the taking up of a place in the world.

Romantic autobiography

The connections between Romanticism and autobiography are close and complex. Many of the autobiographies which come to define the genre for the modern period are written in these decades, though a number were published some years after their composition. In addition to works by Rousseau and De Quincey, autobiographies of the Romantic period include Goethe's *Dichtung und Wahrheit*, Wordsworth's long narrative poem *The Prelude*, and Stendhal's *The Life of Henry Brulard*, written in 1835–6. Memoirs and 'reminiscences', often of other contemporary writers, also flourished at this time, sometimes framed as travel narratives or recollections of place. Such 'records', 'recollections', and 'reminiscences' form a bridge between biography and autobiography in the 19th century. They are also part of a burgeoning commercial literary culture, centred upon the personality, and celebrity, of authors, and they have close ties to journalism.

In the 1970s, when literary theorists took up the question of autobiography as a genre, they turned frequently to Romantic writers for explorations of subjectivity and selfhood, as well as for an understanding of the ways in which the autobiographical self is produced, or inscribed, in writing. In these contexts autobiography intersects with classically philosophical concerns about the nature of the self and the possibility of knowing it. The Romantic self was perceived as a divided, self-contradictory being. The link between the naming of autobiography as a genre at the close of the 18th century and the birth of the concept of the *Doppelgänger*, or 'double' (the term first used by Jean Paul in the novel *Siebankäs* (1796)) is more than accidental. In autobiography, the written self could indeed be said to become a double of, or another to, the self which writes.

The Romantic focus on landscape and nature, including the Sublime (those aspects of the natural world in which we are made to feel its awe-inspiring force and dimension), is also prominently figured in autobiographies of this time. The autobiographical self of the Romantic period is frequently represented as a journeying, wandering subject, communing with his or her own thoughts, but inspired by the natural world. Introspection—the self's dialogue with itself—is, in this context, the birthplace of autobiographical writing: Wordsworth writes in *The Prelude* of 'turning the mind in upon herself'. The divided self can thus be represented as a self in productive dialogue with itself, while autobiography is often represented as a search for a more harmonious or integrated selfhood.

The Prelude (1799, 1805, 1850) describes the stages of its author's life and development—'the growth of the Poet's mind'—moving through childhood, boyhood, and youth. Samuel Taylor Coleridge, to whom much of *The Prelude* is addressed, referred to the poem, sections of which Wordsworth read to him, as a 'Self-biography'; the term most often employed before 'autobiography' became common coinage. Wordsworth expressed some anxieties, in relation to the 1805 version of the poem, about its focus on his own life: it was, he wrote, 'a thing unprecedented in Literary history that a man should talk so much about himself'. Not unprecedented perhaps; but *The Prelude* nonetheless marks a new stage in the writing of poetry and of autobiography.

Augustine's *Confessions* was an important influence on *The Prelude*, but the figure of the spiritual seeker has been changed into that of the Poet, who makes the search for transcendent truths part of his literary vocation. In the writing of the poem, and the tracing of the roots and development of his creative powers, Wordsworth is attempting to restore them; to write himself back into poetry. He is also seeking a language adequate to his turbulent social and political times—the central books of *The Prelude* describe Wordsworth's youthful experiences of London and of revolutionary France—and to the representation of 'The perturbations of a youthful mind'.

Wordsworth's depictions of time and memory anticipate later psychological models of 'the unconscious': the recovery of the past in *The Prelude* is in fact a recreation, in language, of lost time: an observation of 'the ties | That bind the perishable hours of life | Each to the other, and the curious props | By which the world of memory and thought | Exists and is sustained'. Furthermore, the present self is seen to exist at a great distance, or 'vacancy', from the past self, of selves, whose experiences and feelings it has set out to recapture, so that 'I seem | Two consciousnesses, conscious of myself | And of some other Being'. And the search for origins—the origin of the self, the birth of the self as poet—is put into question by his growing perception that such beginnings are either irrecoverable or illusory. 'How *shall* I seek the origin? where find | Faith in the marvellous things which then I felt', Wordsworth asks, as he attempts to describe the sensations and perceptions of his childhood self, at a time 'In which I walked with Nature'. 'Hard task, vain hope, to analyse the mind, | If each most obvious and particular thought, […] Hath no beginning'.

The question of origins—of where the story (of a life) begins—frequently shapes the variants of autobiography's narrative starting-points, from lengthy accounts of ancestry, genealogies, and family histories ('this, or these, are what made me') to representations of the 'birth' of the individual's consciousness and consciousness of self, frequently figured in 'the first memory'. Such footholds on past time are, nonetheless, often shadowed by the knowledge that such starting-points can, ultimately, only be a species of 'make-believe' or necessary fictions.

The transcendental self

Rousseau's final work, *Reveries of the Solitary Walker*, represented solitude as a precondition for meditation, enabling the self's dialogue with itself which was, for Rousseau, the basis of what he described as his 'painstaking and sincere self-examination' and which, more broadly, constitutes what has come to be known as 'autobiographical consciousness'. At the same time, Rousseau expressed a wish to transcend the personal: 'My meditations and reveries are never more delightful than when I forget myself. I feel ecstasies and inexpressible delight when I melt, so to speak, into the system of beings and identify myself with the whole of nature.' This 'transcendental' impulse has also informed a highly significant genre of life-writing, in which the authorial self channels the observation of the external, and usually the natural, world. This self escapes biographical particularities in order to become what the 19th-century American Transcendentalist writer and philosopher Ralph Waldo Emerson called a 'transparent eyeball' absorbing reality: 'all mean egotism vanishes. I become a transparent eyeball; I am nothing; I see all; the currents of the Universal Being circulate through me; I am part or particle of God.'

Many writers and thinkers in 19th-century America, among them Ralph Waldo Emerson, Henry Thoreau, and Walt Whitman, produced first-person writings which lay outside the confessional tradition and did not reconstruct the narrative of a whole life. Emerson wrote of Thoreau that 'he lived for the day, not cumbered and mortified by memory'. While Thoreau does not reach back into the details of his own past in *Walden*, he creates a significant mode of autobiography; one that has helped shape subsequent memoirs and nature and travel writings. *Walden*, Thoreau's account, published some ten years later, of the two years (1845–7) he spent living in a cabin which he built in the woods next to Walden Pond, near Concord in Massachusetts (see Figure 3), brings together his account of the natural world with his philosophy of life. 'I should not talk so much about myself if there were anybody whom I knew as well', Thoreau writes at the book's opening. Knowledge of the world is centred in the observing, experiencing self and the work of the highest value which any writer can produce is, he suggests, 'a simple and sincere account of his own life'.

WALDEN.

By HENRY D. THOREAU,

AUTHOR OF "A WEEK ON THE CONCORD AND MERRIMACK RIVERS."

. . . propose to write an ode to dejection, but to brag as lustily as chanticleer in th morning, standing on his roost, if only to wake my neighbors up. — Page 4.

3. Title page of *Walden*, with illustration of Thoreau's cabin at Walden Pond.

'I went to the woods because I wished to live deliberately', Thoreau writes. His two years at Walden Pond are an 'experiment' in living (recalling the 'self-experiments' described in Rousseau's *Reveries*) and a testing of 'experience'. The terms 'experiment' and 'experience', central to Thoreau's writings as they were to those of Montaigne, Rousseau, and Emerson, share a common root, in the Latin *experior*, 'to try'. There is a connection here with the old

French 'essai' (trial, attempt, essay), which becomes a term for the informal, often digressive, genre of the 'essay' so closely associated with Montaigne and the essayists writing after him. In his essay 'Walking' (1862), Thoreau extols the virtues of 'sauntering': 'you must walk like a camel, which is said to be the only beast which ruminates when walking'.

Walden is in many ways a more rooted text, as Thoreau focuses on his improvised home and his immediate surroundings. He wishes to stand, in his words, 'on the meeting of two eternities, the past and future, which is precisely the present moment: to toe that line'. The text combines details of everyday life and practical circumstance—Thoreau's lists of goods and expenditures recall Benjamin Franklin's 'book-keeping' in his autobiography—with philosophical meditations and practical wisdom. Extolling, like his mentor Emerson, the virtues of self-sufficiency, Thoreau writes: 'the man who goes alone can start to-day; but he who travels with another must wait till that other is ready, and it may be a long time before they get off'. While there are sections of *Walden* in which Thoreau describes his enjoyment of company, his greater commitment is to the importance of solitude, in which state (and as for Rousseau) the self becomes another to itself in the process of 'a certain doubleness'. The splitting Thoreau describes between the experiencing self and a part of the self which stands apart from the self as 'a spectator, sharing no experience, but taking note of it' could also be understood as a definition of the autobiographical act, with its division between the 'I' who writes and the 'I' who is written.

The locus and focus of Thoreau's 'experiment' in living is Walden Pond itself, which alters so dramatically with the seasons, marking, in particular, the change from winter to spring. Thoreau observes the 'depth and purity' of the pond (or lake) and its 'remarkable transparency'. A lake is, he writes, 'earth's eye; looking into which the beholder measures the depths of his own nature'; the depth of human character and the imagining of the infinite are, Thoreau suggests, made possible by the depth and purity of the natural world. An observer may also reflect upon the passage of his or her life, by contrast with the changeless waters: modernity has brought the railroad to the pond's shores but 'it is itself unchanged, the same water which my youthful eyes fell on; all the change is in me'.

As significant to Thoreau as biographical time (his own lifetime), or the times in which he lives, is deep time (natural time, prehistory), into which he seems to look as he sounds the depths of the pond. Of Walden and its neighbouring ponds Thoreau writes: 'How much more beautiful than our lives, how much more transparent than our characters are they!' 'Transparency' is a key term for Romantic autobiographers: in addition to Emerson's image of the ego-less self as a 'transparent eyeball', we find Dorothy Wordsworth, in her *Journals*, repeatedly recording the effects of 'transparency', as perceived in the lakes by her home, as a measure of her own emotions. For Rousseau, whose detractors have seen him as the epitome of egotism, it is in fact 'transparency' which he claims as his ideal state as autobiographer: the merging of the individual self with the natural worlds of water and air. The ego is dispersed into the broader nature of being.

Yet it was also possible to make a virtue of autobiographical self-celebration. Benjamin Franklin wrote at the beginning of his autobiography that vanity 'is often productive of Good to the Possessor and to others that are within his sphere of Action'. The American poet Walt Whitman's 'Song of Myself', in his *Leaves of Grass* (like *The Prelude*, an autobiographical poem revised over many decades), is an unashamed expression of delight in his own human form and energies and in those of others. He is, he writes, a being both complete and at one with all other human beings: 'I resist anything better than my own diversity [...] I am large [...] I contain multitudes.' In *Leaves of Grass*, Whitman does not so much explore personal experience as celebrate life, including the life of the body, depicting each and every life as extraordinary.

Leaves of Grass has been described as a 'vicarious national autobiography', and the question of national autobiography became particularly charged as the 'New World' sought to forge a cultural and historical identity. Walt Whitman also adds to the pastoralism of earlier Romantic autobiography a celebration of urban landscape and experience, in particular that of New York. His vision would have a profound influence on many American writers of the 20th century. In *A Walker in the City* (1951), the first volume in an autobiographical trilogy, the literary critic Alfred Kazin recaptured his boyhood as the son of East European Jewish immigrants growing up in Brownville, a then-impoverished Jewish suburb of Brooklyn. 'To be a Jew', he writes, 'meant that one's very right to existence was always being brought into question.' The autobiography begins with the author's return (which is both literal and an act of memory) to the streets of his childhood, and the re-encounter with their sharp smells: 'an instant rage comes over me, mixed with dread and some tenderness'. Ambivalence is indeed the keynote of Kazin's relationship with the culture from which a life in literature has detached him but which still inhabits him: 'I am back where I began'.

Kazin recalls the intensity of his parents' ambition that he 'redeem the constant anxiety of their existence. I was the first American child, their offering to the strange new God.' His escape from the pressures of family, the school whose values rest on 'Americanism—the word itself accusing us of apparently everything that we were not'—and his own stammering self lies in walking the streets: 'It troubled me that I could speak in the fullness of my own voice only when I was alone in the streets, walking about'. Books, reading, literary characters become one with this 'walking about': 'I learned so well to live with them that I could not always tell whether it was they or I thinking in me'.

A Walker in the City exists in a tradition of Romantic autobiography, taking up the legacies of Emerson and Whitman (lines from whose poem *Crossing Brooklyn Ferry*—'on the walk in the street, and passage over the river'—are its epigraph). It also explicitly invokes the language and sensibility of James Joyce's *A Portrait of the Artist as a Young Man*. Kazin's could be defined as an 'aesthetic autobiography', both in its representation of the redemptive force of literature (as in Edmund Gosse's memoir *Father and Son*, among many other autobiographical works) and (like Vladimir Nabokov's autobiography *Speak, Memory*) in its intensely lyrical, imagistic prose. Yet Kazin does not allow us to forget that this is a language created both to recapture *and* to leave behind the 'tormented heart' of the world in which he grew up.

'Most stories are travel stories', writes the American cultural critic Rebecca Solnit in her 'cultural autobiography' *A Book of Migrations* (1997), her account of travelling in Ireland, birthplace of her maternal great-grandparents, 'and in traveling our lives begin to assume the shape of a story. It may be because a journey is so often a metaphor for life itself that journeying is satisfying... Perhaps if we didn't imagine life as a journey rather than some other metamorphosis—the growth of a tree, for example—roads would not seem like destiny itself, but we do and they do.' *Migrations* is concerned with, in Solnit's words, 'this play between memory, identity, movement, and landscape', using the 'subjective and personal not to glorify my mundane autobiography but as a case study in how one can explore the remoter regions of the psyche by wandering across literal terrain'. As in much modern travel writing (including the work of Jonathan Raban, Paul Theroux, Patrick Leigh Fermor, Jan Morris, and V. S. Naipaul) the story is both that of a journey to place and into the self.

Chapter 3
Autobiographical consciousness

The concepts of time, memory, and identity which are central to autobiographical theory are also perennial concerns of philosophers, who have given widely differing accounts of them, both in their formal philosophical work and in their more personal reflections. A number of these writers, including Giambattista Vico in 1725 and R. G. Collingwood in 1939, explicitly saw themselves writing *as philosophers*, both in their approach and in their subject matter. (As Collingwood described it: 'the autobiography of a man whose business is thinking should be the story of his thought'.) And if one of the purposes of philosophy has often been seen to be a guide to living, the lives of philosophers, whether written by themselves or by others, may also be a source of possible enlightenment.

The idea of the self runs all through this book, but this chapter takes the autobiographies of predominantly Western philosophers—including Descartes, Montaigne, Hume, Nietzsche, Sartre, and Simone de Beauvoir—as central examples, and focuses on their representations of memory, the self in and through time, concepts of subjectivity, identity, and consciousness, and self-formation or 'becoming'. The last theme is most marked in existentialist autobiographies, such as those of Sartre, de Beauvoir, and André Gorz. The chapter also discusses recent theories of 'autobiographical consciousness', including the work of Jerome

Bruner, who has explored the way in which self-narration secures a sense of continuous identity, and Antonio Damasio, who has posited a distinction between the 'core self' and the 'autobiographical self', the latter understood as an 'extended consciousness', which develops throughout the individual's life in relationship to memory and anticipation.

Modern conceptions of the self have been substantially shaped by René Descartes and his immediate philosophical successors. Descartes's *Discourse on Method* (1637) begins with a long autobiographical passage, describing his education and his nine years of travelling before he developed his philosophy. Not until nearly half-way through the book does he present his famous method of doubt in which his certainty about his own existence is based on the fact that he cannot doubt that he is thinking: 'I think, therefore I am (COGITO ERGO SUM)'. After presenting this method and the truths he derives from it, he reverts to an autobiographical mode to describe his reluctance to publish the *Discourse* for some years. Descartes's reflexive approach echoes that of Augustine over a millennium earlier, revived in the course of the Renaissance. A little later, in 1689, John Locke put forward a concept of personal identity based on memory and the continuity of consciousness: 'as far as this consciousness can be extended backwards to any past action or thought, so far reaches the identity of that *person*'.

The analytic philosophy derived from Ludwig Wittgenstein (1889–1951), the Austrian philosopher who settled in Cambridge, generated a more critical approach to what has been described as 'Cartesian privacy', stressing the social nature of language and the impossibility of a private language in which someone could describe their sensations. As the empiricist A. J. Ayer wrote in his autobiography covering his first thirty-six years, *Part of My Life*, 'The great problem . . . is that of avoiding imprisonment in a purely private world.'

The US philosopher Stanley Cavell has attempted to bridge the divide between analytic philosophy and the more speculative approaches, associated with continental Europe and often called 'continental philosophy', which engage more directly with literature. Cavell claimed that 'there is an internal connection between philosophy and autobiography, that each is a dimension of the other'. For Cavell, the close relation between philosophy and autobiography is framed by the classic autobiographical question, 'Who am I writing for?' Cavell quotes Wittgenstein's well-known remark about reaching the limits to philosophical justification and saying 'This is simply what I do.' Autobiographers, one might suggest, say in similar terms, 'This is simply what I have done.' More broadly, as Cavell writes in his autobiography, *Little Did I Know*, the autobiographical dimension of philosophy consists in the fact that 'I speak philosophically for others when they recognize what I say as what they would say, recognize that their language is mine, or put otherwise, that language is ours'.

Narrative identity

As with the notion of Cartesian privacy, Descartes functions more often as a metaphorical reference point than a direct interlocutor. When the neuroscientist Antonio Damasio refers to Descartes' Error, he is rejecting the underlying idea that it is possible to separate the activity of thinking from an awareness of the body, and reason from emotion. He does not refer to Descartes's own venture into what we now call neuroscience in his speculation about the role of the pineal gland, a part of the brain which is now mainly of interest for its secretion of melatonin, with its sedative properties. Descartes serves, however, as a useful peg on which to hang those familiar ideas about mind/body separation. The question frequently asked by philosophers of mind—could what we think of as our experiences just be those of a 'brain in a vat'?—recalls Descartes's speculation that an evil genius might have implanted false beliefs in his mind. Similarly, when Damasio distinguishes in his subsequent book, *The Feeling of What Happens*, between a 'core consciousness' and an 'autobiographical consciousness', he means that the latter includes memories of what we are as well as a core sense of who we are:

> At any given moment of our sentient lives...we generate pulses of core consciousness for one or a few target objects *and for a set of accompanying, reactivated autobiographical memories*. Without such autobiographical memories we would have no sense of past or future, there would be no historical continuity to our persons...The interlocking of core and extended consciousness, of core and autobiographical selves, is complete.

As he notes, this is what William James (1842–1910) was thinking of in his concept of the 'stream of consciousness', and it relates to the early 20th-century social psychologist G. H. Mead's distinction between the 'I', the core ego, and the 'me', the person with a social identity.

A number of psychologists and philosophers have explored this concept of an autobiographical self, arguing either that we tend to see our lives in a narrative form or that we should do, or both. Oliver Sacks, in his book *The Man Who Mistook His Wife for a Hat*, claimed that 'each of us constructs and lives his life as a "narrative"' and that 'this narrative *is* us, our identities'. Bruner, who published his own autobiography in 1983 and whose work in the last two decades of the 20th century was substantially concerned with autobiography, similarly claims that the 'self is a perpetually rewritten story' and that 'we *become* the autobiographical narratives by which we "tell about" our lives'. A 'good story' needs to be judged by other criteria than a scientific explanation. As he wrote a few years later: 'I take the view that there is no such thing as a "life as lived" to be referred to'. A life is created or constructed by the act of autobiography.

The US philosopher Daniel Dennett suggests that 'we...find ourselves engaged in all sorts of behaviour, and...try to make all of our material cohere into a single good story. And that story is our autobiography.' Charles Taylor adds that we *have to* do this as 'a basic condition of making sense of ourselves', as an 'inescapable structural requirement of human agency'. 'A self exists', he writes, 'only within "webs of interlocution"': 'Our modern notion of the self is related to...a certain sense of inwardness.' He traces this sense through Augustine and Descartes who share 'an emphasis on radical reflexivity' and argues that 'by the turn of the eighteenth century, something recognizably like the modern self is in process of constitution, at least among the social and spiritual elites of northwestern Europe and its American offshoots'.

The French philosopher Paul Ricœur, similarly, asks: 'How...could a subject of action give an ethical character to his or her own life taken as a whole if this life were not gathered together, and what other form could it take than precisely that of a narrative?' Taylor and Ricœur converge on the notion that the question 'Who am I?' becomes the question 'Where do I stand?' As Taylor puts it: 'This mode of life-narration...is the quintessentially modern one, that which fits the experience of the disengaged, particular self. It is what emerges in modern autobiography, staring with the great exempla by Rousseau and Goethe.'

These formulations have moved from the factual claim that we often do sort our ideas and representations of ourselves into a narrative form to the claim that we *ought* to do this—thus restating the familiar trope that 'the unexamined life is not worth living'. The first claim seems fairly unproblematic: if someone asks you who you are, a typical response, apart from saying your name, may be to offer a short biographical narrative. The second, normative claim seems more contentious. Unless we are writing our *curriculum vitae*, there seems no essential reason for us to think constantly about our lives in a narrative sequence.

Galen Strawson has long contested a narrative conception of the self:

> I have absolutely no sense of my life as a narrative with form, or indeed as a narrative without form. Absolutely none. Nor do I have any great or special interest in my past. Nor do I have a great deal of concern for my future.

Another British analytic philosopher, Derek Parfit, found a perspective of this kind liberating, contrasting it with his previous view in which he 'seemed imprisoned in myself. My life seemed like a glass tunnel.' This position may be unusual, but Strawson and Parfit are not alone in defending it, and it has important implications for autobiographical theory.

Existentialist autobiography

A philosopher in a very different style, the existentialist Jean-Paul Sartre, famously has his leading character in his novel *Nausea*, Roquentin, say that 'a man is always a teller of tales, he lives surrounded by his stories and the stories of others, he sees everything that happens to him through them, and he aims to live his own life as if he were recounting it'. He goes on, however, to resist this way of thinking and behaving as inauthentic; 'one has to choose between living and narration'. Existentialist autobiography is a subgenre of its own, with Sartre and de Beauvoir writing theirs, Camus's writing displaying strong autobiographical elements, and the American Sartre scholar Hazel Barnes writing one herself, subtitled *A Venture in Existentialist Autobiography* (1997). Michael Sheringham adds to Sartre and de Beauvoir, Jean Genet's *Thief's Journal* (1949), André Gorz's *The Traitor* (1959), and Violette Leduc's *La Bâtarde* (1965), suggesting that 'these do seem to have more in common with each other than with other autobiographies'.

Nausea was published in 1938, marking Sartre's first engagement with the theme of autobiography, and his major work, *Being and Nothingness* (1943), outlined a kind of philosophical basis for it in the section on what he called 'existential psychoanalysis'. The well-known existentialist slogan that 'existence is prior to essence' is directed both against fixed conceptions of human nature as something given (and also in Heidegger's conception of 'thrown-ness' into existence or Marxist social determinism) and against the Freudian model of an ego determined by preconscious desires and drives. We are, instead, the product of our existential choices, for which we are irreducibly responsible. Rejecting the idea that a personality (Sartre uses the example of Flaubert, whose biography he wrote much later) can be explained by a single trait, he suggests instead that the key is an 'original project' formulated by, in this case, Flaubert himself. A biography, or any other account of a personality, has to grasp this 'individual secret' of the person's 'being-in-the-world'. This existential psychoanalysis aims to illuminate 'the subjective choice by which each person makes themselves a person, that is, announces to themself who they are'. The theme is also articulated by Nietzsche in his model of 'becoming what you are'—the subtitle of his autobiography *Ecce Homo*, written in 1888.

Sartre later modified this emphasis on choice, stressing instead the way in which the individual is shaped in childhood and 'tries to act out, without understanding it, the social character imposed on him by adults'. The project is now conceived as the ongoing attempt to go beyond, without completely leaving it behind, this initial conditioning. Sartre himself wrote a biographical essay on Baudelaire (1946), dedicated to Genet, a biography of Genet himself (1952), and his own autobiography, *Les Mots* (*The Words*) (1964), which includes the sentence: 'I detest my childhood and everything which remains of it'. His earlier *War Diaries*, written at the beginning of World War II, but not published until after his death, document his shift towards a greater recognition of external influence on the individual.

Simone de Beauvoir's six-volume autobiography focuses substantially on her childhood, though in somewhat less negative terms, emphasizing her good fortune. She also stresses the theme of the project: 'throughout these years of childhood, adolescence and youth my freedom never took the form of a *decree*: it was the carrying out of an initial project, continually resumed and strengthened—to know and to express'.

The social philosopher André Gorz's *The Traitor* (1957) also centres on the theme of choice, problematizing identity and the act of writing. Gorz makes a classically existentialist assertion: 'whatever happens to me, it is I who happen to myself'. Sartre writes in the foreword to the book: 'You hold in your hands this surprising object—a work in the process of creating its author.'

Sartre's *Words*, first drafted in 1953 but not published until 1964, restates the theme of the half-conscious project, shaped by external historical and cultural forces. 'My true self, my character and my name were in the hands of adults; I had learnt to see myself through their eyes; I was a child, this monster they were forming out of their regrets.' Sartre uses Gorz's theme of the traitor, which he says he became and has remained, repudiating his inauthentic past; 'since about ten years ago I have been a man waking up'. Existentialist autobiographies differ in the degree to which they engage systematically with existentialist philosophy; there is, in fact, more of this in Gorz's than in Sartre's.

French existentialism draws on the philosophy of Hegel and Husserl, but also on a longer tradition which can also be called existentialist and whose most prominent representatives are Nietzsche and Kierkegaard—both highly autobiographical writers. Nietzsche wrote famously in *Beyond Good and Evil* (1886) 'what every great philosophy so far has been: the personal confession of its author and a kind of unintended and unwitting memoir'. His *Ecce Homo* in a sense inverts this, since it interweaves biographical details with summary accounts of his works and their reception. Nietzsche's affirmation of life in his doctrine of eternal recurrence, that we should contemplate with joy the idea of experiences being infinitely repeated, suggests a positive view of autobiographical reflection, though he also warns, in his long essay on the 'advantages and disadvantages of history for life' (1876), that too much retrospection is harmful both for individuals and for peoples and cultures. A whole volume of his collected works is devoted to autobiographical writings, which he began in his teens with a short diary entry entitled 'my life'.

Kierkegaard did not write a formal autobiography, but his *Journals* contain a great deal of autobiographical material and he also wrote three short pieces, two of them published only posthumously, on his work as an author. He published much of his work under pseudonyms, and wrote that he took care to appear a good deal in public so that people would not associate this man about town with the author of his central work, *Either/Or*. More broadly, however, he writes about the anonymity of the modern author: 'one need not inquire about the communicator, but only about the communication, the objective only'. *Either/Or* presents two alternative conceptions of the good life, aesthetic and ethical, both grounded in the principle that 'Every man, however modest his talents, however subordinate his position, feels a natural need to form a view of life, a conception of life's meaning and aim.' The choice between the aesthetic and the ethical is what we would now call an existential one.

Autobiography and identity

The Scottish 18th-century philosopher David Hume (1711–96) wrote a very short autobiography shortly before his death, which stands out for an attitude which is 'philosophical' in the colloquial sense of making the best of things. Describing with good humour the mixed reception of his various books, he concludes with a similarly upbeat account of his final illness:

> I possess the same ardour as ever in study, and the same gaiety in company. I consider, besides, that a man of sixty-five, by dying, cuts

off only a few years of infirmities; and though I see many symptoms of my literary reputation's breaking out at last with additional lustre, I knew that I could have but few years to enjoy it. It is difficult to be more detached from life than I am at present.

A number of philosophers, like other autobiographers, have been motivated to write by the sense that their time was running out. John Stuart Mill feared that he might die of consumption, and Collingwood rightly saw his successive strokes as a warning of his impending death in 1943. The British philosopher Gillian Rose (1947–95) wrote the first of two autobiographical books, *Love's Work* (1995), after being diagnosed with terminal cancer, combining an account of her intellectual development with highly personal reflection. She reveals her illness half-way through the book, after chapters describing her love of an old friend dying of AIDS, a colleague who also died before they could make a planned trip to Israel, and her own lovers. The theme of identity, both personal and social, is central to the book: Jewish, Anglican, philosopher, sociologist, changing her name on her sixteenth birthday from her father's to her stepfather's, navigating transitions from a training in Oxford analytic philosophy to engagement with Adorno and Hegel, law and religion. The first chapter, describing her childhood and family history, is linked with an account of her role on an advisory commission on the memorialization of Auschwitz—itself disputed between post-communist Christian Polish nationalism and Jewish memory.

Hume's conception of identity is a much simpler one. His scepticism about the self, restated in a rather different way by Galen Strawson in the present century, is grounded in his empiricist theory of knowledge:

> when I enter most intimately into what I call *myself*, I always stumble on some particular perception or other, of heat or cold, light or shade, love or hatred, pain or pleasure, I never can catch

myself at any time without a perception, and never can observe anything but the perception.

The chain of associations between our perceptions, he argues, generates our conception of personal identity, but there are no grounds for extending this into a more ambitious conception of the self, still less the religious idea of the soul.

If there is anything distinctive about the autobiographies of philosophers, it is perhaps this link between their conceptions of personal identity and their autobiographical writings. Rousseau describes how his reading of philosophy helped him to understand himself, as well as to develop a set of ethical principles. The empiricist philosopher Bertrand Russell, whose three-volume autobiography combines philosophical, personal, and political reflections, did not, however, address the question of the self in his philosophical work, and his occasional mentions of it are distinctly cerebral. In *Problems of Philosophy* (1912) he writes: 'All acquisition of knowledge is an enlargement of the Self, but this enlargement is best attained when it is not directly sought.'

The philosopher and historian who attributed the greatest importance to autobiography is perhaps Wilhelm Dilthey (1833–1911). He is well known for the remark that 'In autobiography we encounter the highest and most instructive form of the understanding of life.' The 'typical examples' represented by Augustine, Rousseau, and Goethe demonstrate the 'connectedness of life' and a focus on experienced time. Self-understanding is in a sense the cell-form of a broader concept of human self-understanding practised and expressed in history, philosophy, and literature and distinct from the forms of causal explanation found in the natural sciences. The concept of time plays a different role in the two types of science, with the more abstract sense in the natural sciences contrasting in the human sciences with a conception of time as advancing into the future which 'always contains the memory of what has just been present'. In this sense autobiography is a means to understanding the 'specific sense in which the parts of the life of mankind are linked into a whole'. In autobiography, the person who understands the life-course is 'the same as the one who created it. This results in a special intimacy of understanding.'

The social conception of the self and its life which Dilthey derived in part from Hegel is one which has been very prominent, if not dominant, in the following hundred or so years. It can also be found in the North American pragmatist tradition in the early 20th century, in Erving Goffman's studies of what he called the presentation of self in everyday life, through to Michel Foucault's historical analysis of care of the self from ancient Greece to the present, Stephen Greenblatt's concept of self-fashioning in Renaissance Europe, and Judith Butler's conception of gendered and other identities as performance.

The ground for many accounts of self and subjectivity is an understanding of the gradual historical transition whereby conceptions of the 'soul' as a real substance, still lingering on in many religions, give way over time to a secular but still substantial idea of the self. This in turn gives way to a form of life in later modernity where we increasingly see ourselves as forming and choosing our identities, juggling multiple identities rather as we increasingly juggle multiple and fragmented forms of employment and family relations.

Dilthey's conception of autobiography was developed by his son-in-law Georg Misch, by Georges Gusdorf in France, and by a number of autobiographical theorists elsewhere in Europe and North America. The central theme of self-awareness was stressed by Gusdorf and defended by the US critic James Olney against the perceived threat from 'deconstruction'. The deconstructive approach of Jacques Derrida focused substantially on autobiography as an instance of the problematic relation between a life and a text. In one of his first books, *De la grammatologie* (1967), Derrida quoted the way in which Rousseau distanced himself, as he put it in the *Confessions* (Book 6), through writing: 'I only began to live when I contemplated myself as a dead man'.

In a text of 1979, *L'Oreille de l'autre*, eventually published as *The Ear of the Other* (1985), Derrida again addresses the relation between life and death, citing Nietzsche's remark in *Ecce Homo* that 'it is perhaps merely a prejudice that I am alive'. When Nietzsche, as he puts it, 'recounts this life *to himself*', the narration, Derrida suggests, is autobiographical not in the conventional sense but 'because he tells *himself* this life and he is the narration's first if not the only addressee—within the text'.

Deconstructive criticism has stressed the paradoxical relation between autobiographical self-presentation and what Paul de Man called 'de-facement'. There is here a certain parallel with Michel Foucault's stress on the disciplinary use of confession in his history of sexuality. Deconstruction, particularly as it has been taken up in the English-speaking world, pursues analogies between philosophical and literary writing, leaving behind Derrida's earlier concern with the specific features of *philosophers'* autobiographies. Cavell's contributions both to philosophy and to autobiography demonstrate their affinities.

This chapter has focused primarily on individual identity and memory, but there is also a substantial literature on collective memory, whether in a historical or a more immediate form. Such memories, whether real or learned, form an important part of the identity of collectivities such as nations or ethnic communities. Maurice Halbwachs's classic book of 1925 continues to inspire the sociology of memory. More recently, the French-British anthropologist Maurice Bloch has explored the relation between autobiographical memory and more remote historical memory, and between narrative and more episodic conceptions of the self.

The philosopher Henri Bergson, who was a major influence on Marcel Proust, distinguished between what he called the 'pure memory' of conscious recollection and 'habitual memory' (such as remembering how to swim or ride a bicycle). Many collective memories are of the latter kind: a half-conscious awareness of the way 'we' respond to social situations. Bergson's distinction is related to one which becomes increasingly prominent in early 20th-century contexts, between 'involuntary' and 'voluntary' memory. Proust notoriously begins *À la recherche du temps perdu* with the involuntary memory evoked by the eating of a madeleine cake, but goes on to a massive work of voluntary remembrance which nonetheless includes involuntary elements.

In psychoanalysis, too, the voluntary effort to remember is also fuelled by involuntary and previously repressed memories. Richard Terdiman, for whom 'psychoanalysis is our culture's last art of memory', has argued more broadly that the aftermath of the French Revolution generated a 'long nineteenth century' crisis of memory in which there was anxiety both about *too little memory* and *too much*'. This may also be true of the early 21st century, in which disputes over historical memory have become increasingly fraught. Holocaust denial is perhaps the most extreme example, but there are also ongoing controversies over the histories of colonialism, slavery, fascism, and communism. As Michael Sheringham wrote, 'Not only has memory retained its central place in life writing; the diversification of forms of memory has generated new possibilities for investigating the individual and communal past.'

Chapter 4
Autobiography and psychoanalysis

'If often he was wrong and, at times, absurd,' W. H. Auden wrote in his poem 'In Memory of Sigmund Freud', published a year after Freud's death in 1939, 'to us he is no more a person | now but a whole climate of opinion | under whom we conduct our different lives'. And, we might add, the ways in which we write our different lives. Life-writing has been central to psychoanalysis, which created its own form of biographical narrative. The psychoanalytic case study or case history draws upon the dreams and reminiscences of patients to reconstruct their stories. Psychoanalysis has also profoundly shaped autobiographical consciousness. 'One way of thinking about psychoanalysis', writes the analyst Arabella Kurtz, in dialogue with the novelist J. M. Coetzee in a volume titled *The Good Story*, 'is to say that it is aimed at setting free the narrative or autobiographical imagination', though she adds that it is the analyst's role to provide both 'attentive listening' and 'selective comment—on those aspects of a life-story which do not seem to hold, or which seem to hint at the possibility that a more convincing underlying story may emerge'.

While psychoanalytic theories and therapies have led to new ways of thinking and writing about the self, psychoanalytic thought also takes up much earlier models of the mind and identity. As in the case of Rousseau, the focus is on the formative nature of childhood experience, in particular in relation to sexual desire.

The concept of an unconscious mind, whose contents are not fully available to the conscious self, but make themselves felt in our dreams and words and through our 'symptomatic' actions, is glimpsed in Augustine and visible in the writings of Romantic autobiographers, including Wordsworth and De Quincey.

On the occasion of his seventieth birthday Freud was greeted as the 'discoverer of the unconscious', but he corrected the speaker: 'The poets and philosophers before me discovered the unconscious. What I discovered was the scientific method by which the unconscious can be studied.' The poets and philosophers on whom Freud drew most substantially for quotation and insight were Romantic thinkers. As the American critic Lionel Trilling observed, we should not be surprised that Romantic thought and literature was so important for the 'science' of psychoanalysis. Romantic literature was, in Trilling's words, itself scientific, in 'the sense of being passionately devoted to a research into the self'—and, we could add, extensively drawing on the scientific knowledge of its time.

The beginnings of psychoanalysis, as a theory and a practice, can be dated to the mid-1890s, with the term 'psychoanalysis' coined in 1896. Freud's 'self-analysis', on which he embarked in the summer of 1897, was central to its formation and, more specifically, to the dream theory which he expounded in his masterwork *The Interpretation of Dreams* (1899/1900), which centred on the concept of dreams as 'wish-fulfilments'. In Freud's model (later revised to accommodate the traumatic dreams associated with the experiences of World War I), dreams represent disguised and repressed wishes. The process of interpretation in analysis will work back from the 'manifest' dream content (the dream narrative as it is experienced and remembered) to the 'latent', or unconscious, dream thoughts.

Whereas many early dream theorists and interpreters had understood the dream as prophetic of the future, Freud sought to understand its relation to the dreamer's past, both recent and remote. The dream is thus understood (as it was for Thomas De Quincey) as a form of autobiography, and in his self-analysis Freud turned to his own dreams and memories as he formulated many of the fundamental tenets of psychoanalysis, including the Oedipus complex (the child's desire for the mother and jealousy and hatred of the father). In *The Interpretation of Dreams*, Freud used his own dreams as examples, overcoming, as he wrote, 'some natural hesitation about revealing so many intimate facts about one's mental life'. The dream-book has come to be seen, as it was by Freud himself, as his true autobiography, by contrast with *An Autobiographical Study*, in which he recounts the course of his professional and intellectual rather than his 'inner' life.

In one of his letters from 1897 to his friend and fellow physician Wilhelm Fliess, Freud wrote that he had come 'to the definite realization that there is no "indication of reality" in the unconscious, so that it is impossible to distinguish between truth and emotionally-charged fiction'. Freud's blurring of the boundaries between truth and fiction has been troubling in relation to its original context: the apparent recall, by his predominantly female patients, of 'perverse acts by the father', which he came to understand as 'sexual phantasy'. Recent years have seen the publication of numerous memoirs whose authors have sought to make their traumatic childhood experiences known and believed. It should be noted, however, that in Freud's theories 'emotionally-charged fiction' is given due significance as a shaping force in the individual's mental life. This has profound implications for autobiographical writings, giving further credence to the idea (which we encountered in relation to Romantic autobiography) that there is a truth of 'feeling' (or 'fantasy') as well as of 'fact', and an 'internal truth', the truth of the self, which will almost certainly run on different lines to those of a veridical or juridical 'external truth'.

Freud further explored ideas of the constructed nature of memories in his 1899 essay 'Screen Memories' (the term indicating concealment) and in the 1907 edition of *The Psychopathology of Everyday Life*. In the earlier essay, Freud examined the phenomenon present in our memories of childhood whereby 'the essential elements of an experience are represented in memory by the inessential elements of the same experience'. Freud's explanation is that the 'indifferent memories' of childhood are substitutes for more important impressions. The example at the heart of the essay is, in his translator and editor James Strachey's words, 'autobiographical material only thinly disguised'. Freud recounts one of his own memories as if it were that of another. The remembered 'scene' from childhood turns out, on analysis, to have displaced later 'mental experiences' which remain 'almost unconscious'. 'It may indeed be questioned', Freud writes, whether we have any memories at all *from* our childhood: memories *relating to* our childhood may be all that we possess'.

In the later discussion of 'screen memories', Freud focuses on childhood 'memories' in which 'the essential thing with which the memory is occupied *precedes* the screen memory in time'. The 'screen memory' is a displaced version of the earlier, 'essential', event, historical or mental. Freud also points to the intense visuality of childhood memories: 'In these scenes of childhood, whether in fact they prove to be true or falsified, what one sees invariably includes oneself as a child, with a child's shape and clothes'. The childhood self is seen as a figure from outside, as opposed to memories or impressions seeming to arise from the perspective of an inside looking out.

In this discussion of 'screen memory', as in the earlier essay, Freud turns to one of his own memories, but this time in undisguised form. He refers to it as a 'scene which had for a long while back (from the remotest past, as it seemed to me) come into consciousness from time to time'. The 'scene' played a central part in Freud's self-analysis of 1897, as his letters to Fliess from this time show, leading towards his 'discovery' of '[the phenomenon of] being in love with my mother and jealous of my father' which, he wrote, he now considered 'a universal event in early childhood'. Freud thus 'finds' the Oedipus within himself, universalizes the 'complex', and then returns it to the self as a question of empathy and identification: 'the Greek myth seizes on a compulsion which everyone recognizes because he has felt traces of it in himself'.

Freud's fascination with childhood memories led him to a brief analysis of an episode in Goethe's autobiography *Dichtung und Wahrheit*. (Freud interprets the remembered 'scene', in which the young Goethe throws the household crockery out of a window, in relation to the child's response to his mother's pregnancy and the sibling rivalry he experienced.) Here autobiographical material is used as the basis for analysis. This was greatly extended in Freud's 'case study' of the psychosis of Judge Schreber, which was based not on any actual encounters with Schreber, but on the memoir (*Memoirs of My Nervous Illness*) which Schreber wrote, while incarcerated in an asylum, in an attempt to reclaim his legal and civic rights.

Freud produced a lengthy analysis of a childhood dream of Leonardo da Vinci's in his first 'psychobiography', *Leonardo and a Memory of His Childhood*. 'We must lay hold of biography', he wrote to his one-time friend, the analyst Carl Jung, in the early years of psychoanalysis. The impact of Freudian thought on the genre of biography was profound in the early and middle decades of the 20th century. It reached its heights with the psychoanalytically informed 'new biography' of the 1920s and 1930s, the mid-century 'existential psychoanalysis' of Jean-Paul Sartre, who produced biographies of Gustave Flaubert and Jean Genet, and the 'ego-psychology' which, flourishing in the US in the 1950s, led to such biographical works as Erik Erikson's *Young Man Luther: A Study in Psychoanalysis and History* and *Gandhi*, and Bruce Mazlish's study of James and John Stuart Mill. In these texts the focus was on the self as a developing identity and its adaptations to the world.

Psychoanalysis has also been a shaping force on 20th-century autobiography, though its impact here is in many ways harder to pin down than in the case of biography. For some biographers at least, psychoanalysis became a totalizing method of interpretation, and they would frequently focus upon some defining incident or personal trait which was perceived to shape the whole of a life. Few autobiographers have felt able, or wished, to analyse themselves in this way, and many have indeed expressed antagonism towards psychoanalytic explanations. Nonetheless, the influence of psychoanalysis on autobiography reveals itself in a number of crucial ways, direct and indirect.

It is felt very fully in 20th-century autobiographies' observations and representations of the partial and often flawed nature of memory, and suggestions that there might be experiences in the life which are at once profoundly important and nonetheless lost to recall. There is an understanding that we are impelled by fears and desires which we do not fully comprehend, and which are not under our control. Arthur Koestler, whose autobiography of his early years, *Arrow in the Blue*, expresses some scepticism towards psychoanalysis and its interpretations, concurs with Freud's assertion 'that apparently irrelevant facts yield the most important clues'. 'Thus', Koestler writes, 'the selection of relevant material is a highly problematic affair, and the crux of all autobiography'.

Autobiographies require narrative and structure to be readable, but for psychoanalysis 'free association', the articulation of the (ideally) uncensored flow of memories, imaginings, and ideas as they come into the mind, is understood to be the method by which our most fundamental thoughts, wishes, and defences are revealed. There have been a number of autobiographies which seek to transmit the play of thought and speech in the psychoanalytic session, though such strategies have been criticized by, among others, the psychoanalysts Adam Phillips and J. B. Pontalis. Pontalis argues that it is not possible 'to transpose spoken free associations into writing—the sudden recalls, the transferential shifts, the repetitions and the discontinuities of discourse'. Writing, in Pontalis's view, is always a *transformation* of 'primary process'.

Yet 20th-century autobiography has been profoundly and, it could be argued, productively shaped in the following of the path of memories as they emerge to present consciousness, as opposed to their more conventional shaping into a linear time sequence. French writers Roland Barthes and Michel Leiris rejected chronology, instead organizing their autobiographical texts around dominant themes, images, dreams, and fantasies. In Leiris's case, these are markedly erotic and sexualized. At the close of his autobiography *Manhood*, he writes of what he has learned from psychoanalysis: 'one is always identical with oneself, that there is a unity in a life, and that everything leads back, whatever one does, to a small constellation of things which one tends to reproduce, in different forms, an unlimited number of times'. Here the unity of the self, for so long a cultural ideal, is perceived as a product of a set of obsessions and, in Freud's phrase, a 'compulsion to repeat'.

Psychoanalytically informed understandings of identity move between concepts of the self as multiple and divided and/or as unified by patterns established in the early years of life. The British psychoanalyst Charles Rycroft observed of autobiography that, while we might speak of the autobiographer and the subject as 'by definition the same person', in fact neither 'are single selves but are rather multiple sets of selves…The appropriate visual analogy ceases to be that of a painter painting a self-portrait and becomes that of someone occupying a temporal corridor of mirrors and communing in turn with images of past and present selves.' Modernist author Katherine Mansfield, thinking of her 'Freudian' age, wrote in her journal of the impossibility of observing the prescription 'To thine own self be true': 'True to oneself! which self? Which of my many—well really, hundreds of selves?', though she also suggested that 'the rage for confession, autobiography, especially for memories of earliest childhood' might be explained by 'our persistent yet mysterious belief in a self which is continuous and permanent'. For Pontalis: 'One shouldn't write *one* autobiography but ten of them or a hundred because, while we have only one life, we have innumerable ways of recounting that life (to ourselves).'

Freud or Jung?

Freud and Jung parted company conclusively in 1913. In his own autobiography, *Memories, Dreams, Reflections* (written in collaboration with Aniela Jaffé), Jung suggested that sexuality for Freud had taken the place of the religious impulses he had outwardly rejected. *Memories, Dreams, Reflections* contains a chapter entitled 'Sigmund Freud', in which Jung describes the many differences of opinion and belief between them. Dreams and dreaming were a fundamental issue. Jung rejects Freud's account of the dream as a *façade* concealing repressed materials, and argues for dreaming as 'a part of nature'.

In *The Interpretation of Dreams* Freud describes a dream in which he was dissecting his own body. He interprets the self-dissection as a figure for his own self-analysis, 'linked up with my giving an account of my dreams' and related to questions of mortality and of one's own death, towards which all life leads but which cannot be a dimension of narrated experience. The dream is not only part of an autobiography, but becomes a way of representing the autobiographical, or self-analytical, act.

Jung's version of the dream–autobiography relationship comes in the chapter in his autobiography on 'Sigmund Freud'. He describes a dream in which he is in a house, which he knows to be his own: he ventures into its lower storey, and finds a much older house, with a stairway leading down into an ancient room. Here there is another stairway, descending into a low cave, with broken pottery and scattered bones, 'like remains of a primitive culture'. The dreamer finds two ancient human skulls, and then awakes. Freud, on being told the dream by Jung, returned repeatedly to the question of the two skulls, clearly seeking, Jung writes, for an interpretation in which they would represent secret death wishes.

Jung's own interpretation, which marks the development of his separate branch of psychoanalytic thought, which he termed 'analytical psychology', is that 'the house represented a kind of image of the psyche' and that the lower levels of the house stand for the deeper levels of the unconscious, with the cave holding 'remains of a primitive culture, that is, the world of the primitive man within myself'. The dream led, Jung writes, to his understanding of a 'collective unconscious' (a concept at the heart of Jungian thought), which lies beneath the 'personal psyche' and which finds its form in dreams, myths, and legends. From this storehouse of material emerges the individual's 'personal myth'.

Both Freud and Jung, in their different ways, entered into periods of self-exploration which formed the bases of their life's work. Dreams and their meanings were central to this. Freud undertook a 'self-analysis', while Jung spent a period of years 'pursuing my inner images'. Throughout the years of World War I, Jung undertook, as he writes, his 'experiment in confrontation with the unconscious'. The understanding he gained, he wrote, was that there is no 'linear evolution' to the self, but only a 'circumambulation'. Everything points not towards an end goal but 'towards the centre'.

The search for the 'personal myth', so central to Jung's thought, shaped the work of a number of 20th-century autobiographers. The Orkney-born poet Edwin Muir wrote, in *An Autobiography* (the first part of which was published as *The Story and the Fable* in 1940): 'There are times in every man's life when he seems to become for a little while a part of the fable, and to be recapitulating some legendary drama which, as it has recurred a countless number of times in time, is ageless'. In the early decades of the 20th century in Britain, when Muir (like Mansfield) was starting out on his literary path, Freud's and Jung's theories were discussed from every angle in the journals of the day. 'The conception of the unconscious', Muir writes, 'seemed to throw new light on every human problem and change its terms'.

In 1920, Muir started analysis with Maurice Nicoll, who was sympathetic to Jungian thought. Soon after beginning the analysis, Muir writes, 'my unconscious mind, having unloaded itself, seemed to have become transparent, so that myths and legends entered it without resistance and passed into dreams and daydreams'. Muir describes at length a particular waking dream, or vision, he had at this time, and his continued belief that 'it was not "I" who dreamt it, but something else which the psychologists call the racial unconscious, and for which there are other names'. Muir's visionary experiences at this time recall his accounts of his Orkney childhood, a world in which 'there was no great distinction between the ordinary and the fabulous'. His professed belief in immortality 'seems to be connected with the same impulse which urges me to know myself'. In writing his particular 'story', Muir as autobiographer also reaches out towards an unending 'fable', and dreams provide one of the passages between the two orders of reality.

Psychoanalysis in autobiography

Muir's autobiography is one of a number of significant works in which the experience of psychoanalysis forms a part of the life-story which is being explored and narrated. Other examples include the American poet H.D.'s memoir *Tribute to Freud*, in which she recalls her two periods of analysis with Freud in the Vienna of the 1930s. H.D. shares with Muir a conviction that the vivid waking dream she experienced was not a 'symptom' (as Freud saw it) but an 'inspiration': she is critical of Freud's 'materialism' but nonetheless writes a 'tribute' to the great man and his methods. She uses archaeological imagery to represent the relationship between the classical and Egyptian artefacts in Freud's study and the contents of mind and memory: 'there are priceless broken fragments that are meaningless until we find the other broken bits to match them'. *Tribute to Freud* is at once intended to suggest the processes of 'free association' and crafted to represent the ways in which patterns are both found and made.

The art historian Adrian Stokes went into analysis with the Austrian-born analyst Melanie Klein in 1930. His experience of psychoanalysis resulted in two autobiographical works, *Inside Out* and *Smooth and Rough*, which the philosopher Richard Wollheim described as like the intricate work of a goldsmith. These were the first texts in which Stokes fully used psychoanalysis, as if he, like Freud, felt that he could only incorporate its discoveries once he had, as Wollheim writes, 'confronted them with his own experience and seen their necessity'. Stokes's accounts of his past are shaped by Kleinian theories, as he represents the different spaces occupied in childhood and youth in relation to Klein's models of the destructive and reparative stages of early development. Describing the landscapes of his early life, Stokes writes that 'Hyde Park is especially a destroyed and contaminated mother, Italy the rapid attempt to restore'.

In his own autobiography, *Germs: A Memoir of Childhood*, Wollheim traces patterns of association in his childhood fears and fantasies, pursuing his philosophical understanding of autobiography as 'a literary genre singularly dedicated to the notion of pattern in life or the idea of wholeness... It is poised between the writing and the rewriting of a life.' We may either rewrite our lives malignly, giving to that life a unity it never possessed, or benignly, 'so as to achieve, even at a late hour, some reconciliation with the past'.

In *Germs*, Wollheim refers only briefly and obliquely to his analyst, 'Dr S', but his invocation of this figure nonetheless reminds the reader that the memories and episodes recounted in the text have already passed through the processes of speaking, listening, and interpreting entailed in psychoanalysis. The autobiography points to the important, though complex, relationship between the identities of autobiographers and analysands, and between analysts and readers.

Adam Phillips has suggested that psychoanalysis might be seen as a prelude to autobiography (rather than being identical with it). This is certainly the case for the historian Ronald Fraser, whose autobiographical text *A Search for the Past* alternates accounts of his analytic sessions with those of the interviews he conducted with the servants on the country house estate where he grew up. The intention was to explore the past through two different lenses: those of social history, in which he would look at his childhood and family through the perspectives of others, as objective 'evidence', and his past as he had lived and experienced it, with the processes of analysis unlocking buried memories. At the close of the text, the dialogue between analyst and analysand expresses agreement over the relationship between the inner world which psychoanalysis explores, and the evidential basis of history: between 'subject' and 'object', 'inside and out'.

The model of the 'inside out' has been a central one for autobiography, suggesting an exploration of the autobiographer's inner world which is then turned outwards, through writing and towards a readership. Some works of psychoanalytic autobiography have, however, been more fully focused on complex and troubled interiorities which resist translation into conventional modes of life-writing. Marie Cardinal's autobiographical novel *The Words to Say It* represents the different selves—'the mad one', 'the sick one'—which not only inhabited her during her long period of psychotic illness but with whom she also learned to live after its end. On the analyst's couch, 'I began to speak of my mother, never stopping until the end of the analysis. Over the years I explored the depths of her being, as though she were a dark cavern. Thus did I make the acquaintance of the woman she wanted me to be.' Both the analysis and the writing of the autobiography are understood as acts through which she can become, in the analyst Bruno Bettelheim's words, 'mistress of herself'. In broader terms, there has been an extension of psychoanalysis as the 'talking cure' (the term coined by one of Freud's earliest patients) to the concept of the 'writing cure', or 'scriptotherapy', which is underpinned by the belief that the 'writing out', and 'writing through', of difficult or traumatic experiences, and the composition of an integrated life-story, will have powerful therapeutic effects.

It was the aim of psychoanalysis, Freud wrote, to reduce unbearable neurosis to ordinary unhappiness. This pessimistic, or perhaps realistic, account of the human condition has found expression in the tragi-comic modes of some psychoanalytic autobiography. The film-maker Woody Allen has for many years exploited the black humour of modern neuroses. Essayist Adam Gopnik and critic and translator Dan Gunn convey the frustrations of patients 'paying through the nose', as Gunn puts it, for lengthy periods of silence: 'Analysis isn't free, and association isn't free either, because, quite simply, you pay and pay', Gunn writes, in his *Wool-Gathering or How I Ended Analysis*. One of psychoanalysis' most significant contributions to autobiography might indeed be, as Gunn's memoir suggests, an opening out to the absurd (not as the ridiculous, but as the terrain beyond rationality) in writing as in life.

Chapter 5
Family histories and the autobiography of childhood

'My true self, my character and my name were in the hands of adults; I had learnt to see myself through their eyes; I was a child, this monster they were forming out of their regrets.' So writes Jean-Paul Sartre in *Les Mots*. Opening with a family history and family legends, Sartre depicts the ways in which fathers have sought to make their sons in their own, or their preferred, image. Echoing (and ironizing) Freud's assertion that the most significant event of a man's life is his father's death, Sartre writes of his own father's death, which occurred soon after Sartre's birth, that it 'was the great event of my life: it returned my mother to her chains and it gave me my freedom'.

Growing up with his young, widowed mother and her parents, the young Sartre becomes the family miracle: 'My mother and grandmother often invited me to repeat the act of outstanding goodness which brought me into the world [...] I would be hidden behind a piece of furniture [...] my grandfather would come into the room, tired and depressed, just as he would have been had I not existed; suddenly, I would emerge from my hiding-place and do him the favour of being born'. Staging and restaging his own birth, Sartre was, as the adult autobiographer represents his childhood self, an imposter, a play-actor in the family romance. Yet, without a father, he has the freedom to invent, or to author, himself.

The years of childhood have become increasingly central to autobiographical writing. Historians have linked this development to the new ideas about life-stages which emerged in the early modern period. Philippe Ariès (1914–84) made a key contribution in 1960 with a book on the child and family life in the *ancien régime*, known in English as *Centuries of Childhood*. Arguing against the conception that family life had deteriorated in modernity, he suggested that in fact it was only around the 17th century in Europe that the idea of childhood as a distinct life-stage emerged. Prior to this, he claimed, children above the age of seven were generally seen as small adults and the idea of the relatively private, child-centred family is a recent one. Ariès used a wide variety of artistic and literary sources, including memoirs of childhood, though he also suggested that memoirists are not typical: 'the ordinary man does not write his memoirs'.

Genealogy—the tracing of family history—has been for many centuries a starting point for autobiographers. The 18th-century historian Edward Gibbon, whose incomplete *Memoirs of My Life* was begun in 1772 and published in full in 1815, opens his autobiographical narrative with a chapter on 'Family History'. Gibbon finds particular interest in tracing his lineage, though he also suggests, in ways which run counter to the democratizing principles of contemporary family history, that 'the longest series of peasants and mechanics would not afford much gratification to the pride of their descendant'.

Gibbon also suggests a relationship between 'biography' (life-writing) and 'biology' (life-science or life-knowledge, the term coined at the very start of the 19th century), as he points not just to the fact of his birth but also to his actual emergence into the world: 'Decency and ignorance cast a veil over the mystery of generation, but I may relate that after floating nine months in a liquid element I was painfully transported into the vital air'. Thereafter, his account of youth is predominantly focused on the stages of learning and education (with a brief paragraph given over to the death of his mother when he was nine), and his making, or moulding, at university in Switzerland: 'Such as I am in genius or learning or in manners, I owe my creation to Lausanne. It was in that school, that the statue was discovered in the block of marble.' The freedom to pursue an 'independent life' follows from his father's death in 1770: Gibbon emphasizes his filial affections, but observes that 'The tears of a son are seldom lasting...It is a melancholy truth, that my father's death, not unhappy for himself, was the only event that could save me from a hopeless life of obscurity and indigence.'

The relationship between the philosopher John Stuart Mill and his father James Mill—historian, political economist, and educationalist—occupies a central place in Mill's autobiography: his mother receives no mention. Like Gibbon's *Memoirs*, Mill's *An Autobiography* is the 'record of an education' and, though his formation is very different to that of Wordsworth, also an account of 'my early mental development'. Mill's teacher was his father, who 'demanded of me not only the utmost that I could do, but much that I could by no possibility have done'. The method of instruction included Mill's tuition in Greek from the age of three onwards. Mill emphasizes the great gains given by his education, but also notes the limitations of his father's philosophy (influenced in part by Benthamism), with its relative indifference to pleasure and to the realms of emotion and feeling. The promotion of fear as a means of educating the young serves, Mill suggests, 'perhaps to seal up the fountains of frank and spontaneous communicativeness in the child's nature'.

In 1826, when Mill was twenty-one, he entered a period of depression or, in his term, 'dejection'. 'The fountains of vanity and ambition seemed to have dried up within me, as completely as those of benevolence', he writes, extending the metaphor of the 'fountains' of communicative and affective life. His mental condition began to improve, he writes, when he chanced upon the 18th-century French historian Marmontel's *Memoirs*. Of the passage in which Marmontel relates his father's death, his family's subsequent suffering, and his determination, as a young boy, to become 'the man of the house', Mill writes: 'A vivid conception of the scene and its feelings came over me, and I was moved to tears. From this moment my burthen grew lighter. The oppression of the thought that all feeling was dead within me, was gone. I was no longer hopeless: I was not a stock or a stone.' The 'tears' represent the flow of the formerly sealed or dried up 'fountains'. Mill does not comment on the fact that the 'scene' Marmontel describes is that of a son taking the place of, or displacing, his father.

Mill's understanding of the importance of 'feeling' and of the need for attention 'to the internal culture of the individual' become closely connected to his increasing valuation of poetry and art, connections cemented when in 1828 he read Wordsworth's poems for the first time: 'They seemed to be the very culture of the feelings, which I was in quest of'. This new sensibility, which Mill represents as opposed to his father's models of education and his philosophy, is at one with his autobiographical act, with its focus not only on intellectual, public, and collective life (which certainly forms a very substantial part of the text) but also on the need to 'penetrate inwards'.

Mill's pained but respectful depictions of the differences between the generations take sharper form in Edmund Gosse's 1907 memoir *Father and Son*. Gosse's text (initially published anonymously) represents his break, as a young man, with his father's beliefs and values as an impassable divide between not only generations but also 'epochs'. Gosse, who would become a highly influential literary critic and commentator in the late 19th and early 20th centuries, was the son of Philip Henry Gosse, an eminent Victorian scientist who found himself torn between his religion (he belonged to the strict Christian sect the Plymouth Brethren) and the intellectual appeal of evolutionary thought, which radically undermined the doctrine of Creation. Gosse's narrative lies somewhere between autobiography, biography, and memoir and depicts scenes and dialogues in ways which indicate the increasing, or renewed, proximity between fiction and auto/biography in the early 20th century. In discussion of the problems of writing autobiography, Gosse wrote: 'A very great difficulty is to select. My own view is that one ought to take certain vivid passages as samples or examples, elaborate them into living pictures, and entirely omit other passages of no less interest.'

A central thread of the narrative is Edmund's gradual turning away from the religion of his childhood towards literature. (Many Plymouth Brethren were extremely hostile to fictional writing, on the grounds that it told 'untruths' about the world.) The youthful Gosse's 'turning to literature' (which echoes Mill's salvation through his reading of memoir and poetry), and away from 'the artificial edifice of extravagant faith', is represented in a language of 'conversion' which echoes, rewrites, and, ultimately, subverts the powerful conversion moment in Augustine's *Confessions*: 'it was as though the light of confidence flooded into my heart and all the darkness of doubt was dispelled'.

Father and Son ends with Gosse on the threshold of his new life. He ends his story as his young adult self enters into (productive) time (rather than, like Augustine, moving out of linear or narrative time into timelessness). He represents his father, who continued to deny the logic to which evolutionary science would have led him, as one of a dying species. Biographers and autobiographers writing in Gosse's wake would understand him to have performed an act of symbolic parricide (the killing of the father) which was, in turn, inseparable from the ways in which 'the moderns' would seek to differentiate themselves from their Victorian predecessors.

The hybrid nature of Gosse's *Father and Son*—both and neither an autobiography of the son and a biography of the father—is repeated in more recent autobiographical writing which has explored family relationships. J. R. Ackerley's *My Father and Myself* is a search for the hidden truths of the father's life through which the son can gain an understanding of his own sexual identity. Martin Amis interweaves passages from his father Kingsley Amis's *Memoirs* into his autobiography *Experience*. Blake Morrison's *And When Did You Last See Your Father?*, a modern classic of the father–son relationship is, like Amis's, a more affectionate portrait than many, but it too uncovers family secrets; including the badly kept 'secret' of his father's long-term adulterous relationship with a woman known to the family as 'Auntie' Beaty. The father's death is, for Morrison, as momentous an event in his own life as Freud maintained, and the memoir moves between scenes of his father's months of dying, with all its physical indignities, and episodes revealing the robust and irrepressible father—a country GP—with whom he grew up.

If the 'parricide' in Gosse's *Father and Son* was entirely symbolic—the 'killing' resting on the way in which the new generation replaces the older one—it comes close to being a literal act in the Scottish poet and novelist John Burnside's *A Lie about My Father*. Burnside's feelings towards his abusive, alcoholic father form the central thread of the narrative: they come to a head when, as a teenager, Burnside meets his father's aggression with a kitchen knife: 'What he must have seen […] was the look of pure hatred on my face; a look which, all of a sudden, had finally revealed to us that, whatever the cost, I would have been quite happy to kill him'. When the father's death (of a heart attack) finally comes, it is little more to Burnside than a confirmation of the emotional absence that has defined his relationship to him from the outset.

'For my father, and for whole generations of working-class men, cruelty was an ideology', Burnside writes. 'What he wanted was to warn me against hope, against any expectation of someone from my background being treated as a human being in the big hard world. He wanted to kill off my finer—and so, weaker—self. Art. Music. Books. Imagination. Signs of weakness, all.' The damage done by this ideology of 'masculinity', defined in large part as an absence, or rejection, of the world of feelings, is at the heart not only of Burnside's memoir but also of many autobiographical works focused on the father–son relationship. Other recent examples include the Irish novelist John McGahern's *Memoir*, in which he recounts his beloved mother's death in his childhood and the violence he and his siblings endured at the hands of their remaining parent, and the actor Alan Cumming's account of his brutal father in *Not My Father's Son*.

This focus extends, for all the differences in time and circumstance, the accounts of the paternal rejection of the worlds of feeling, literature, and imagination given by Mill and Gosse. The very writing of an autobiography—the weaving of words in the recounting of a life and its relationships—becomes part of that world of feeling and imagination which had been suppressed or denied. This world is often associated with the figure of the mother, whose marriage is a source of suffering for her and with whom the son identifies.

It is, however, the world of imagination which may touch dangerously on the duplicitous story-making and self-mythologizing that can destroy the self's grounding in reality. Burnside's father's 'lies' were part of his self-construction as a man. A 'foundling, a throwaway', in Burnside's words, he endlessly fabricated stories about himself and his past: 'My father told lies all his life, and because I knew no better, I repeated them. Lies about everything, great and small, were the very fabric of my world.' While the autobiographical basis of his text is not in question, Burnside implicitly troubles both the issue of autobiographical truth and the nature of filiation when he writes: 'This book is best treated as a work of fiction. If he were here to discuss it, my father would agree, I'm sure, that it's as true to say that I never had a father as it is to say that he never had a son.'

The American novelist Paul Auster's *The Invention of Solitude*, begun in the weeks after Auster's father dies, represents the process of coming to terms with the shock and finality of death. It is also focused on the father as a man 'absent' during his own life. Emptying out his deceased father's house, the family home before his parents' divorce, Auster finds an expensively bound photograph album, with the lettering 'This is Our Life: The Austers'. It was 'totally blank inside'. *The Invention of Solitude* expresses a desire to recuperate something, in words and memories, from the failed relationship between father and son. Like Burnside, Auster ends with an image of his own young son, as if to suggest that the negative and destructive patterns of filiation might at last be broken. These autobiographers seek to show that they are their son's fathers rather than their father's sons.

'There's always a danger with childhoods that weren't perfect: trying to tell the story truthfully can feel like an exercise in sentiment', Andrew O'Hagan writes, in his essay 'Guilt: A Memoir'. He suggests that writers might survive their childhoods rather better than others: 'A writer romances the truth and invents his own freedom. My childhood can never let me down as a guide to human complication.' O'Hagan continues:

> The most popular picture round our way—every family had one—usually above a three-bar fire—was a commercial painting called *The Weeping Boy*. There were several versions of it, but they all showed a child in distress. I believe it helped us to visualise our self-pity, and to accept a certain amount of kitsch. I spent hours looking at that picture, thinking it odd, thinking it mawkish, but feeling it must be social realism.

The category of the 'misery memoir', sometimes known as 'pathography', indicates both the commercial structures of publishing which have promoted the literature of 'the imperfect childhood' and a certain contempt for, and perhaps exhaustion with, such writing. The category of 'misery literature' seems to have first been used to describe the American writer Dave Pelzer's memoirs of his abusive childhood with an alcoholic mother; these, in particular the first, *A Child Called 'It'*, remained bestsellers for a number of years. Pelzer's writing brings together graphic accounts of intense childhood suffering with an insistence that such a past can be survived; in addition to his autobiographies, Pelzer has written a number of works of self-help and life-coaching.

The 'misery memoir' is, however, too broad and generalized a label to do justice to the range of autobiographical works, and ways of writing, that might conceivably fall within its purview. Frank McCourt's *Angela's Ashes*, an autobiographical account of an impoverished childhood, first in New York and then in Ireland, was also a major commercial success, but it takes an ironic distance from 'pathography'. As McCourt writes: 'When I look back on my childhood I wonder how I survived at all. It was, of course, a miserable childhood: the happy childhood is hardly worth your while. Worse than the ordinary miserable childhood is the miserable Irish childhood, and worse yet is the miserable Irish Catholic childhood.' Andrea Ashworth's *Once in a House on Fire* tells, in prose at once harsh and lyrical, the story of a childhood spent under the domination of two 'unfathomably violent' stepfathers. Her survival and escape, too, come through books and through her own words: 'I could put poetry into clouds and gutters and all kinds of filth. I could turn nasty things at home into stories.'

Jeanette Winterson's memoir, *Why Be Happy When You Could Be Normal?*, returns to many of the persons and scenes described in her semi-autobiographical first novel *Oranges Are Not the Only Fruit*, in which she gave a vivid account of an eccentric childhood. Her narrator is, like Winterson herself, the adopted daughter of working-class Pentecostal parents in the North of England; the extraordinary, terrifying mother is the force from which she must escape. More than two decades later, Winterson writes in the memoir that *Oranges*—'faithful and invented, accurate and misremembered, shuffled in time'—was a 'cover version' of her childhood experiences: 'I wrote a story I could live with. The other one was too painful. I could not survive it.' She uses the language of trauma, while suggesting that the 'wound' is closely allied to the 'gift': 'All my life I have worked from the wound. To heal it would mean an end to one identity—the defining identity. But the healed wound is not the disappeared wound; there will always be a scar. I will always be recognisable by my scar.' Winterson connects the 'wound' to her birth mother's pain in giving her up, as a six-week-old baby, for adoption.

'Adopted children are self-invented because we have to be; there is an absence, a void, a question mark at the very beginning of our lives', Winterson writes. The memoir raises many questions which are important for our understandings of identity and of life-writing: the relationship between novel and memoir/autobiography, fact and fiction, the distortions of memory, the invention of the self, and the damage done by the lies which are told to children. As the writer Hilary Mantel puts it, in her autobiography of childhood, *Giving Up the Ghost*:

> When you were a child you had to create yourself from whatever was to hand…disinformation, or half a tale, and much of the time you probably put the wrong construction on what you picked up. How then can you create a narrative of your own life? Janet Frame compares the process to finding a bunch of old rags, and trying to make a dress.

Truth, secrets, and lies are also at the heart of Mary McCarthy's *Memories of a Catholic Girlhood*, a memoir which has led to much critical discussion of the unreliability and distortions of memory, and the necessarily partial or contested nature of autobiographical truth.

Family relations

The 1960s and 1970s saw radical changes in historical studies, with, in Britain in particular, a major turn towards working-class and women's history. In some European contexts, a number of historians moved towards the history of everyday and private life, turning to archives which frequently included first-person narratives. The new social history emphasized the relationship between private lives and cultural structures, giving new value to the first-person narration of 'ordinary lives', while also perceiving them as a route into an understanding of broader social formations. Many working-class autobiographies from the 19th century were republished, community publishers promoted the writing and dissemination of new life-stories, and 'oral history' (in which life-stories are narrated and recorded) became a significant historical vehicle. Family history and stories of childhood were not the exclusive focus of this work, but they became an important strand, as they are in the 'refugee stories' emerging from the crises brought about by war, exile, and displacement in the 21st century.

Childhood (a South London 1950s childhood) in the historian Carolyn Steedman's *Landscape for a Good Woman* is placed in a broader social history; that of working-class women's experience in particular. Social class is, for Steedman, a decisive, defining, and divisive factor. Gender, too, is a shaping force. 'This book', she writes at its opening, 'is about lives lived out on the borderlands, lives for which the central interpretative devices of the culture don't quite work'. In *Landscape for a Good Woman* Steedman is concerned not only with her personal story, nor that of her mother, but with the untold stories of such marginal lives. 'This is a sad and secret story', she writes of her mother's life, 'but it isn't just hers alone'.

The literary scholar Lorna Sage's *Bad Blood*: *A Memoir* is more fully focused on the particularities of her family history, in all its eccentricity, though it also takes place against the backdrop of a changing post-World War II Britain. Sage's autobiography takes her from an early childhood in a village on the Welsh borders, almost unchanged since the 19th century, where her grandfather was the vicar. Her grandparents live in the gloomy vicarage in a state of 'mutual loathing', along with, in the war years, Sage's mother and herself, while her father is away fighting. It is Sage's grandfather who teaches her to read before she is four: 'This confirmed me as his creature'. Books and the world of literature are represented by Sage, as by so many autobiographers, as the means of escape: both into the imagination, during an often fraught childhood, and out and away from background and home.

The background to Sage's growing up could not, on the face of it, be more different from that of Simone de Beauvoir's bourgeois Parisian upbringing, as she recounts it in *Memoirs of a Dutiful Daughter*. Yet there are significant connections between the two texts, and their vivid accounts of a young girl's formation. Both writers represent their young selves as combining rebellion against the family with powerful intellectual ambition. And both represent the close female friends of their teenage, or young adult, years as twin or fellow selves. Sage's relationship with Gail is a 'mutual obsession', but one overtaken by events; for Beauvoir, her friend Zaza's life, in a family more conventional and restrictive than her own, and her early death represent the destiny which she has herself escaped. In the closing lines of the autobiography (the first of six volumes) Beauvoir writes: 'We had fought together against the revolting fate that awaited us, and I thought for a long time that I had paid for my own freedom with her death'. This 'fate' is the path that might have been taken—a woman's life in which freedom was not achieved—and this ghost-life is one for which there would have been no autobiographical account; a double silence.

While the shaping of family relations by cultural and social forces has been a central concern for many modern autobiographers, it takes on particularly sharp definition for those who are situated in between, or have crossed, cultures. In *Meatless Days: A Memoir*, Sara Suleri embroiders vignettes of her Pakistani father and Welsh mother as she and her siblings grew up in, among other places, Lahore. She writes of what it means to live with two languages, English and Urdu—'it entails the problems of maintaining a second establishment even though your body can be in only one place at a time'—and describes herself as a 'two-faced thing' with 'ambidextrous eyes'.

The borders between fact and fiction, reality and dream, often become porous as the autobiographer moves between cultures and languages. This 'revisionary' mode of autobiography has been particularly prevalent in non-Western and postcolonial texts, including Gloria Anzaldúa's *Borderlands/La Frontera* and Assia Djebar's *Fantasia: An Algerian Cavalcade*. The Chinese American writer Maxine Hong Kingston's *The Woman Warrior: Memoirs of a Girlhood Among Ghosts* represents a childhood caught between conformity to American values and the power of her mother's stories and their mythic legacies: 'To make my waking life American-normal, I turn on the lights before anything untoward makes an appearance. I push the deformed into my dreams, which are Chinese, the language of impossible stories.'

Some autobiographers only write about their childhood; others pass over it more rapidly in order to focus on their adult life. Gibbon suggests ironically (and pre-psychoanalytically) that his early years cannot have been very different from 'the common history of the whole species... according to a just computation we should begin to reckon our life from the age of puberty'. For Wordsworth, by contrast, 'the child is father of the man', and for the moderns, the years of childhood are likely to be at the heart of autobiographical representation.

Chapter 6
Public selves

While autobiography is often associated with the private and personal, there are many examples which focus less on individual experience, or on self-exploration, than on the nature of the times in and through which the writer has lived. This is the case for the literature of 'witness' discussed in Chapter 1 and, more broadly, for the numerous autobiographies and memoirs in which the primary concern is with cultural transformations, including those which have, over the last century, most affected the lives of women and sexual and ethnic minorities, and/or historical and political events. The autobiographical 'I' becomes a traveller through, and at times a guide to, wider cultural and historical forces, as the individual life-course intersects with, and is shaped by, collective events and experiences. The rise of theoretical interest in autobiography in the final decades of the 20th century, and the growth in the writing of explicitly politicized autobiographical texts, was an integral part of the 'identity politics' of the same period, while the feminist slogan 'the personal is the political' proved a spur to life-writings by women (among them Kate Millett, Maya Angelou, and Gloria Steinem) whose stories were both particularized and placed within broader contexts and struggles.

The autobiographies of public figures known for their political, intellectual, cultural, or sporting accomplishments also form an important subcategory of the autobiographical genre, which typically aims to combine the personal and the public. The novelist and former political activist Arthur Koestler thematized this combination in his 1954 autobiography as that between the 'Chronicler's urge' to record external events and the '*Ecce Homo* [behold the person] motive' of presenting personal experience. The proportions vary, though the public events tend to predominate, with the personal confined to a limit set by the author's conception of what the reading public might be or ought to be interested in. The poet Stephen Spender suggested that public figures 'may really appear to themselves just as they appear to other people... If there is anything left over... that is themselves, it is either unpublishable or else a charming proof to others of their humanity.'

Autobiographies charting the rise and rise of public figures accelerated from the 19th century onwards, allied to the increasing importance of the 'self-made man'. The autobiography becomes the written version of this self-manufacture. Texts by powerful late 19th- and early 20th-century industrialists such as the Scottish-born Andrew Carnegie (written 'in collaboration' with Samuel Crowther) and the American Henry Ford chart life-stories in which there is a move from relative poverty or obscurity to enormous wealth and influence but, in Carnegie's case in particular, it is the connection rather than the contrast with origins that is drawn. As Carnegie (who created some 2,500 'Carnegie Libraries' between 1888 and 1929) wrote of his father, who founded the first public library in Dunfermline, Scotland: 'I had never heard of a lineage which I would exchange for that of a library-founding weaver'.

This chapter focuses on various categories of public autobiography: the life-writings of politicians, those of 'public intellectuals' (individuals mainly known for their cultural or academic achievements but also intervening in public life and current controversies), and celebrity autobiography, which is frequently 'ghosted' by a writer paid to work for and/or with the celebrity, and to produce a 'first-person narrative'. At times, the writer's contribution will be acknowledged (as in the case of the writer Alex Haley's work with the Black activist and politician Malcolm X); more often, the contribution of the 'ghost' is not made visible.

Political and public lives

Records of 'res gestae' ('deeds done') in the Roman period, and accounts of political and military activities, take us back to the beginnings of life-writing, constituting a counter-tradition to the spiritual autobiography associated with Augustine and his followers. Julius Caesar's *De Bello Gallico* (*On the Gallic War*) is an account of the Gallic wars and of the campaigns he commanded, and of the culture of Gaul. Like Xenophon's *Anabasis* (a narrative of campaigns in ancient Greece), it is written in the third person, allowing for (seemingly disinterested) praise and promotion of Caesar as a great military and political leader. Third-person narrative also characterizes the autobiographical writings of the 15th-century Pope Pius II and, more recently and in more ironic vein, *The Education of Henry Adams*, the autobiography of the writer and historian, son and grandson of US political leaders, who charts his progress from the secure *milieu* of 'Boston Brahmins' through the rapidly changing conditions of the modern world. Adams narrates his life as if he were a historian writing a biography of 'Henry Adams'.

Politicians of all stamps and from many national contexts have produced autobiographical works. The memoirs of US presidents include those by Ulysses S. Grant (the record of his life up to the end of the Civil War) and Martin van Buren. The most recent is Barack Obama's acclaimed *Dreams From My Father*, first published over a decade before his presidential election. Obama suggests that the connection between private and public themes, and the idea of a story at once individual and representative, was a motivating force in the writing of the autobiography:

> I ... went to work with the belief that the story of my family, and my efforts to understand that story, might speak in some way to the fissures of race that have characterized the American experience, as well as the fluid state of identity—the leaps through time, the collision of cultures—that mark our modern life.

Obama's Kenyan father, who had met his white American mother in Hawaii in 1960, left in 1963 when Obama was two, with only a brief visit when he was ten, so his presence was mediated primarily by stories told by his mother and grandparents. Obama reflects that: 'all the stories of my father ... said less about the man himself than about the changes that had taken place in the people around him, the halting process by which my grandparents' racial attitudes had changed'.

For an autobiographer who remains active in public life, the stakes of self-revelation are higher. Obama writes of overcoming 'a stubborn desire to protect myself from scrutiny' in composing *Dreams From My Father*. Obama's second book, *The Audacity of Hope*, written in 2006 when he was ten years into his political career, is much less personal. For an active political figure, the demands of image management are likely to shape even the most private reminiscences, and this may conflict with the expectation that nothing important should be passed or glossed over.

Political autobiographies frequently intersect with the personal diary or journal on which many of them are based. The incorporation of diary entries into an autobiographical narrative may serve to smooth out the tension between the personal and the political and to structure the interplay between contemporaneous and subsequent reflections, as well as certifying the authenticity of the autobiographical narrative. Where the public figure is also a writer, the diary may be planned from the outset for publication, as in the case of the British politician Tony Benn, who meticulously tape-recorded a narrative of the day's events, as well as ancillary material such as interviews.

In cases where the writer has played a central role in public affairs, autobiography and history will often begin to merge. Winston Churchill's history of *The Second World War* includes, of necessity, considerable autobiographical material, whereas his 'true' autobiography, *My Early Life*, written in middle age, deals primarily with his earlier years. The focus on early life is common to many autobiographies of major public figures, including Goethe's *Dichtung und Wahrheit*, which he began writing in 1811 but whose narrative ends in 1775, when he was only twenty-six. The close relation, as in Goethe's case, between autobiography and the Bildungsroman is one possible explanation.

Like other autobiographers, public authors often record their ambivalence about telling their story. Koestler notes that he had been trying for fifteen years to write his autobiography: 'I forced myself to go on because I suspected that my loathing for the job, my revulsion against turning an autobiography into a clinical case-history, was due to moral cowardice.' In the 'Author's Note' to his second volume of autobiography, *The Invisible Writing*, he writes of the early chapters of the book, describing his life as a communist in Berlin and the Soviet Union, admitting that he 'found it impossible to revive the naïve enthusiasm of that period: I could analyse the ashes, but not resurrect the flame'.

Nelson Mandela, in his *Long Walk to Freedom*, stresses the exterior impetus from his prison comrades to write an autobiography which 'could become a source of inspiration for young freedom fighters'. Václav Havel, in *To the Castle and Back*, writes: 'I was unable, nor did I wish, to write a full-blown memoir, but after everything I have lived through, I felt I owed people an account of some kind.' The Lithuanian American anarchist and feminist Emma Goldman (1869–1940) wrote a lengthy

autobiography recounting her activism, her imprisonment
in 1893–4 for 'incitement to riot', and from 1917 to 1919
for campaigning against conscription, her subsequent deportation
to the Soviet Union, and her 'enforced European inactivity'
in France. Having previously thought that she could wait until
she was much older and 'capable of viewing the tragedies and
comedies of life impersonally and detachedly', she later decided
to write while she was still able to do so. Like many, however,
she stressed that she was responding to the suggestions of others
that her story should be told.

The Italian Marxist intellectual Antonio Gramsci (1891–1937)
included much autobiographical material in his letters both
before and, more particularly, during the imprisonment which
ended his life, and addressed the topic of autobiography in his
Prison Notebooks, including an 'Autobiographical Note' of 1933.
For Gramsci, autobiography was not necessarily narcissistic,
and it could stress the life as one example among many, whereas
'autobiographism' plays on its putative uniqueness.

Malcolm X's autobiography, which is structured as a 'conversion'
narrative, invokes the importance of the representative life in
autobiographical writing, as well as the continuity in Black American
autobiographical writing, including works by W. E. B. DuBois,
James Weldon Johnson, Richard Wright, and James Baldwin. For
these writers, to whose names we could add Angela Davis and bell
hooks, their personal histories are part of a collective one. As
Obama wrote, in the Introduction to *Dreams*, of people's confused
responses to his 'mixed-race' heritage and the racial politics of
the US: 'the tragedy is not mine, or at least not mine alone, it is
yours, sons and daughters of Plymouth Rock and Ellis Island, it
is yours, children of Africa'.

The writers of memoirs or autobiographies will frequently be
figures whose active public life has ended, so that they have only

their reputations and not their future careers to worry about. One of the most dramatic autobiographical revelations of recent times came in the novelist Günter Grass's autobiography *Peeling the Onion*, in which he revealed that in the last months of World War II, at the age of seventeen and having volunteered two years earlier to serve in the navy, he ended up in the Waffen-SS. The shock was not so much at the fact of his service as a trainee tank gunner, in which he says he never fired a shot, as that Grass, who had made his name with *The Tin Drum* (1959), had constantly condemned West Germany's decades-long failure to address Nazi war crimes and mercilessly criticized any hint of nationalism before, during, and after German unification in 1990. In June 2007 Grass published a lengthy autobiographical article in the *New Yorker* recounting this episode. In interviews, he stressed that he had in fact spoken to journalists in the 1960s about his war service, without attracting attention, and that he had always intended to write about it, but in his own time. Its concealment, he wrote in *Peeling the Onion*, was the result of his feelings of shame.

Many 20th-century autobiographies have emerged from the experience of extreme political and historical events, including those of war and exile. Prominent in the US was the Palestinian literary scholar Edward Said, whose autobiography, *Out of Place*, written shortly before his death from leukaemia in 2003, deserves particular attention here. Although Said's 'memoir', as he described it, ends with his doctoral studies and graduation, the five years he spent writing it coincided with the early years of his treatment. The title refers partly to his exile from Palestine but also to the fact that after nearly forty years in New York 'I still feel away from home'. This is not, he stressed in an essay written around the same time, a matter of identity, 'about as boring a subject as one can imagine...We have to defend peoples and identities threatened with extinction or subordination because they are considered inferior, but that is very different from aggrandizing a past invented for present reasons.'

Ghost-writing and celebrity autobiography

The term ghost-writing was introduced in the US in 1921 by the sports writer Christy Walsh, who launched the Christy Walsh Syndicate of ghost-writers. Many autobiographies of public figures are in fact ghost-written, whether or not this is acknowledged. *The Autobiography of Malcolm X* is explicitly subtitled *With the Assistance of Alex Haley*, and the copyright was assigned to Alex Haley and Malcolm X, though Gary Younge writes in his Foreword to the 2007 edition that 'It is a story that may have been narrated to Haley but was truly written by Malcolm X'. It therefore occupies an intermediate category between an autobiography which just happens to have been dictated, and perhaps edited, and a fully ghost-written text.

In his Foreword to the book, Haley describes their sometimes tense relationship in detail. Malcolm X read through the text, not long before his political assassination, and Haley ends his Foreword with Malcolm X's remark as he signed the contract: 'A writer is what I want, not an interpreter'. Other public figures have attempted to conceal the ghost-writing of their autobiographies. As a Senator, J. F. Kennedy won a Pulitzer Prize for a book of essays substantially co-written by his speechwriter Ted Sorensen: the transition from speechwriter to ghost-writer merits further study.

Tony Blair presumably wrote his own account of his 'ten years as prime minister', which he introduces thus: 'There is only one person who can write an account of what it is like to be the human being at the centre of that history, and that's me.' He was, however, the subject of a novel by Robert Harris, *The Ghost* (2008), about the relationship between an exiled British former prime minister accused of war crimes and his ghost-writer. *The Unauthorised Autobiography* by Julian Assange is a real-life instance, described by Andrew O'Hagan in his essay 'Ghosting'. O'Hagan took on the assignment partly because of his 'sense that the world might be more ghosted now than at any time in history' and his 'instinct to walk the unstable border between fiction and non-fiction, to see how porous the parameters between invention and personality are'. O'Hagan sums up the increasingly fraught relationship with Assange: 'He thought I was his creature and forgot what a writer is, someone with a tendency to write things down and perhaps seek the truth and aim for transparency.' The journalist Decca Aitkenhead describes her much more positive experience of 'ghosting' the autobiography of the footballer Rio Ferdinand. Any difficulties she encountered arose from her subject's emotional reticence and his 'shocking' memory: 'Football had left little space in his head for anything else'. The writing of the book came readily, however, and Aitkenhead suggests that the 'better term for the role I have played would not be ghost but surrogate writer'.

The people we have come to call celebrities are often 'famous for being famous'. The use of the noun celebrity, like autobiography, dates from the early 19th century, but the idea of celebrity or notoriety (Charlotte Brontë referred in *Villette* to 'notorieties and celebrities') has been a feature of discussion of what we now call autobiography since at least the 18th century, when prominent celebrity memoirs were written by, among others, actresses and courtesans, such as Harriette Wilson. Critical discussions of the term have noted the predominance of celebrities working in the entertainment industry (including sport), the emphasis on their private rather than professional activities, and the fact that their lives are frequently presented in terms of chance and luck. More broadly, celebrity has become democratized, though aristocrats remain potential celebrities by birth and what has been called 'achieved' celebrity can also be manufactured.

Celebrity biographies and autobiographies may be written by the celebrities themselves or ghost-written by one or more assistants. One way of making the category more precise is to focus on people either whose celebrity has created a demand for an autobiography or, alternatively, who believe, or are told by their agents or other advisors, that having an autobiography written would cement or augment their celebrity; one commentator suggested distinguishing between 'somebody' and 'nobody' memoirs.

Hollywood in the 1920s saw a dramatic rise in the production of the celebrity autobiography, as the studios realized the commercial potential of their stars. As early as 1919, Dorothy Parker published a satire titled 'The Autobiography of Any Movie Actress, Set Down in the Regulation Manner' and including the splendid lines: 'I have never had time to write, although it has always been my ambition. Ever since I can remember, I have felt that "the pen is mightier than the saw".' Autobiographies of Hollywood stars have proliferated since these early years.

Celebrity autobiographies tend to be written against the principle that autobiographies should be written relatively late in life. Increasingly, perhaps, young celebrities are writing or 'writing' them as part of their self-promotion. Sporting autobiographies may be under particular time-pressure where the sporting career tends to be short, and, like those of ex-politicians, also benefit from speedy publication. The late-life retrospective coexists with the youthful 'first autobiography', as the divisions which purists have attempted to draw between autobiography, memoir, and gossip become ever more blurred.

Public figures may welcome or regret their public prominence, or be media-hounds posing as the hounded. Some gain additional attention for their renowned reclusiveness, with an autobiography or authorized biography acting as the equivalent of the official photo opportunity designed to discourage intrusive paparazzi. The poet W. H. Auden famously wrote that 'Private faces in public places | are both wiser and nicer | than public faces in private places', but also that 'No one likes to feel himself forgotten'.

One way of making sure one is not forgotten is by making even the most obscure and private lives public through social media, notably through blogs and systems like Facebook. Whereas earlier projects linked to social history or anthropology/sociology, such as Mass-Observation in Britain in the late 1930s and 1940s (revived in the 1980s), had, like documentary cinema, recorded the lives and narratives of 'ordinary people', we now increasingly do this for ourselves, informing a potentially unlimited audience of our daily activities and thoughts. If the 20th century came to celebrate everyday life as a serious object of study, the 21st has made mass observers or 'informal collaborators' in self-surveillance out of us all.

Chapter 7
Self-portraiture, photography, and performance

The French scholar Michel Beaujour, in *Miroirs d'encre* (*Mirrors of Ink*) (1980), contrasts the narrative autobiography with the autobiographical 'self-portrait', which represents the author as 'what I am, not what I have done'. Beaujour's examples of the literary 'self-portrait' (which other critics have termed 'autography', or 'self-scripture') include Cardano's *De vita propria*, Montaigne's *Essays*, Rousseau's *Reveries*, Nietzsche's *Ecce Homo*, and, in the 20th century, André Malraux's *Antimemoirs*, Michel Leiris's *Manhood* and *La Règle du jeu*, and Roland Barthes's *Roland Barthes*. All of these works, Beaujour argues, have a thematic rather than a narrative structure, a kind of unfinished self-portrait 'in ink'.

For Beaujour, the 'pictorial metaphor' should not be taken too literally: 'The self-portraitist does not "describe" himself as the painter "represents" the face and the body which he sees in the mirror'. Nonetheless, there are significant relationships between the visual and the literary self-portrait. From classical antiquity onwards, with the philosopher Plotinus' essay on self-portraiture, the suggestion has been that the visual artist, like the literary autobiographer, turns inwards to find his or her self-image, rather than merely representing the mirrored self. 'Withdraw into yourself and look', Plotinus writes. For the artist and art critic Julian Bell,

'Self-portraiture is a singular, in-turned art. Something eerie lurks in its fingering of the edge between seer and seen.'

Images of seeing and mirroring are central to autobiography. Rainer Maria Rilke, in the semi-autobiographical *Notebooks of Malte Laurids Brigge*, written in the early 1900s, writes: 'I am learning to see...I have an inner self of which I was ignorant.' Robert Folkenflik suggests that 'one can think of autobiography itself as a mirror stage in life, an extended moment that enables one to reflect on oneself by presenting an image of the self for contemplation'. W. H. Auden expressed such a relationship much more sceptically, raising the issue of autobiographical deception and self-deception, when he wrote: 'An honest self-portrait is extremely rare because a man who has reached the degree of self-consciousness presupposed by the desire to paint his own portrait has almost always also developed an ego-consciousness which paints himself painting himself, and introduces artificial highlights and dramatic shadows.'

In the Preface to his *Essays*, Montaigne addressed his reader, writing that the intended audience for his 'honest book' was a private rather than a public one. 'Had it been my purpose to seek the world's favour', he writes, 'I should have put on finer clothes, and have presented myself in a studied attitude. But I want to appear in my simple, natural, and everyday dress, without strain or artifice; for it is myself that I portray.' Montaigne thus denies that his self-presentation is a performance, a 'studied attitude', while using the language of self-portraiture to define his writerly task: 'I give my soul now one face, now another, according to which direction I turn it'.

He is by no means alone among autobiographers in using the language of the artist. Life-writing (biography and autobiography) has, throughout its long history, been defined in visual terms: portrait, picture, sketch, impression. The term 'self-portraiture' arises at around the same time (the beginning of the 19th century) as 'autobiography'. Prior to this, the term used for what we now call the self-portrait—'a likeness of the artist by his own hand'—paralleled that of autobiography as 'the life of a man told by himself'. The autobiography in its totality is often represented as an image of the author. Rousseau, in a discarded preface to the *Confessions*, wrote of wishing to give his readers something like a comparison piece to their self-knowledge: 'and that other will be me'. It can be argued, however, that the diary is even closer to self-portraiture than the autobiography in the immediacy and 'momentaneity' of its self-engagement.

The relationship between visual and literary self-portraits is mutual. Portraiture and self-portraiture in art have frequently been linked to biography and autobiography. This is true in particular of serial representations, as in the sequence of over eighty portraits of himself that Rembrandt painted or drew at different stages of his life, from youth to old age. These have often been described as Rembrandt's autobiography. By contrast with Montaigne's expressed wishes for his book, Rembrandt frequently represents himself in costume and 'studied attitude'. As the art critic Laura Cumming writes, 'Rembrandt, young and old, is always in performance' (see Figure 4). Nonetheless, he shares Montaigne's sense of the self—always changing, infinitely complex.

The lives of artists

In 1550, the Florentine artist and historian Giorgio Vasari published *The Lives of the Most Excellent Painters, Sculptors and Architects*. This told the story of Renaissance art through the biographies of many of the principal Italian artists of the time. *The Lives of the Artists* (as it is better known) is often described as the foundational work of modern art history, creating a strong (though by no means uncontested) link between the history of art and the lives of artists.

4. Rembrandt van Rijn, *Self-Portrait, c.*1663.

Since Vasari's time, there have been numerous biographical
studies of artists, but far fewer autobiographical works. By
comparison to those of writers and actors, the record remains
sparse, though 'artists' books' (which may include diary entries,
visual images, sketches, and other gathered material) undoubtedly
have an autobiographical dimension. There is, however, a powerful
example of narrative autobiography from the Renaissance in
Benvenuto Cellini's *Autobiography*, which he wrote at intervals
between 1558 and 1566, though it was not published until 1728.
'No matter what sort he is, everyone who has to his credit what
are or really seem great achievements, if he cares for truth and
goodness, ought to write the story of his own life in his own hand;

but no one should venture on such a splendid undertaking before he is over forty', Cellini writes. His opening words in fact qualify the phrase 'in his own hand'. He had started in such a way on his *Autobiography*, but 'it took up too much of my time and seemed utterly pointless'; he had therefore found a boy to whom to dictate 'my Life', while he carried on with his work. This is his life's work; the hand is fitted not for writing but for the craftsmanship and artistry of the goldsmith and sculptor.

Cellini's *Autobiography* is a picaresque narrative, in which the story of its author's coming to fame as an artist is intertwined with the power politics of Renaissance Italy and with his own reprobate acts. Its climactic episode is the account of Cellini's casting of his bronze statue *Perseus with the Head of Medusa*, commissioned by his patron Duke Cosimo I (see Figure 5). Cellini describes in detail the making of the wax model of the Perseus, its clothing in a clay mould, and the construction of the furnace. As the fire burns, Cellini is, as he describes it, smitten with a deadly fever but, on hearing that the casting process is failing, springs from his bed to save the situation, saying: 'Before I die I'll leave such an account of myself that the whole world will be dumbfounded'.

As the clotted metal becomes molten again under his ministrations, he saw that 'I had brought a corpse back to life [and] was so reinvigorated that I quite forgot the fever that had put the fear of death into me'. The next stage is the removal of the cast from the bronze statue to reveal its near perfection. Throughout the dramatic scene, Cellini stages reanimations; of the metal, the statue, and his own fevered body. The Perseus statue is, like his *Autobiography*, Cellini's 'dumbfounding' account of himself and on the back of Perseus's helmet he moulded his own self-image.

There are only a few published artists' autobiographies between Cellini's *Autobiography* and those appearing in the 19th century. These include works by the painter Benjamin Robert Haydon, the Pre-Raphaelite artists and chroniclers of the Pre-Raphaelite

5. Cellini's *Perseus with the Head of Medusa*.

movement Holman Hunt and William Michael Rossetti, and the artist and art critic John Ruskin. The impressionist painter Vincent van Gogh's letters to his brother Theo have also been defined as a work of autobiography: in penning his daily letters to Theo, van Gogh was, in Irving Stone's words, writing 'the story of his own life'.

Ruskin, the most celebrated writer on art and architecture of the Victorian age, wrote his autobiography *Praeterita* in the 1880s. Ruskin's is an 'impressionist' autobiography, focused less on events than on things seen: from the close-up views of childhood—'the carpet, and what patterns I could find in bed covers, dresses, or wall-papers to be examined, were my chief resources'—to his later journeys in Europe and more particularly in Italy. When Ruskin travels to Rome with his parents they commission a 'cameo' of their son, who finds his image in profile much less pleasing than the 'front face' he is used to seeing in the mirror. Of the cameo portrait, 'as also other later portraits of me', he writes, 'I will be thus far proud as to tell the disappointed spectator, once for all, that the main good of my face, as of my life, is in the eyes'. Ruskin's is a life given over to vision.

'Ekphrasis' is a term denoting the use of written language to describe a visual work of art. The autobiographies of artists and art critics of necessity use words to recreate the visual dimension of their worlds. As the art historian Michael Baxendall put it in his autobiographical work *Episodes: A Memory Book* (published in 2010, two years after its author's death): 'the fact remains that visual art is behaviour in shapes and colours, and—short of dancing or painting it—art criticism's language is in a different relation to visual art'. In artists' and art theorists' autobiographical works, experience is often organized around space rather than time, and spaces and spatial relationships are seen to shape the individual's inner life and sense of identity.

The late 19th-century classicist and aesthete Walter Pater opened his sketch 'A Child in the House' with his autobiographical persona's dream of the house where he had lived as a child: 'this accident of a dream was just the thing needed for the beginning of a certain design he had then in view, the noting, namely, of some things in the story of his spirit, in that process of brain-building by which we are, each one of us, what we are'. In *Episodes*, Michael Baxendall dwells on the attic rooms which he occupied as a teenager: 'I cannot summon up a very clear image of all the attic, nothing like a photograph, but the plan of it is something, or is part of something, in which I suspect I still move'. As the analyst J. B. Pontalis writes, in his autobiography *Love of Beginnings*: 'Memory is less subject to time—that enigma—than to space, which gives it shape and consistency...Our memory is a *camera obscura* or, more prosaically, a box-room where useless remnants hide, where blazing splinters flare up: the disparate objects in a timeless attic.'

Photography, identity, and memory

With the advent of photography in the early 19th century a new and heightened relationship between text and visual image emerged. This was by no means without anxiety, and a repeated theme was that photography, with its inability to select from the details that come into view, was having a negative effect on literary and artistic representation, pushing both towards an 'inartistic' and unselective realism or naturalism. We also see an increasing concern, particularly relevant to autobiographical contexts, about the ways in which photography might be replacing memory: what we think we recall may not in fact be a 'memory image' but a 'photographic image'.

From the early decades of the 20th century onwards, autobiographical texts, like biographies, have routinely included a set of photographic images, providing visual representations of the writing 'I' and a visual narrative of the life being recorded. A photographic series depicting the author from early to later life represents the evolving, changing, ageing body and the different life-stages of the authorial self, as a counterpart to the chronological narratives of many autobiographical texts. There are, of course, differences: photography provides a record of the self at a particular moment, or moments, in time, by contrast with the retrospective narrative mode of most autobiographical texts. Autobiography and photography share, however, a 'referential' quality, a 'truth to life', which is perceived to differ from that of fiction or painting.

The emergence of photography as a technology followed closely upon the 'naming' of autobiography as a genre distinct from biography. Photography also came to be used as a way of documenting identity. As the listing of the autobiographer's name as the author of the book was taken (as theorized in Philippe Lejeune's writings on autobiography) to secure the identity of the writer and the subject, so the conjuncture of a photograph and an officially registered name was taken as a proof of identity. Photographic identity documents were issued to exhibitors and employees at the 1876 Centennial Exposition in Philadelphia, though passports and other identity documents with photographs did not come into general use until around World War I.

The possibility of 'seeing yourself as others see you' in the early decades of the photographic medium (the claim that would later be made for film in its first years) almost certainly played its part in shaping literary self-representations. On the one hand, photography could be said to have produced a new form of self-consciousness and hence a sharper divide between biography and autobiography: the representation of the self is perceived to differ radically from the depiction of another. On the other, it may in fact have blurred this divide, precisely because the self in the photograph is seen as another, as if from the outside. In recent years, this form of externalization has been realized in 'graphic' life-writings (by, among others, Art Spiegelman and Alison Bechdel), which have become particularly popular modes of self-representation in Chinese and Japanese contexts. The 'frames' of the cartoons depict sequences of life-events, while the drawn figures depict the self both alone with his/her thoughts and in interaction with others, as articulated in the written narration and dialogue accompanying the visual image.

The autobiography of the literary and cultural theorist Roland Barthes, *Roland Barthes by Roland Barthes* (whose title indicates the mirrored and doubled relationship between the autobiographer and his/her subject) explores the perception of the self as other through visual means. In the first pages of his text, Barthes offers a series of visual images: 'the author's treat to himself, for finishing his book'. The photographs are family portraits, images of houses and places, portraits of the author as a baby, child, young man, and adult. The captions include reflections on photography and identity. Barthes writes that 'I never look like myself', but also finds in the images of himself as a child 'not the irreversible' (lost time) but the 'irreducible: everything which is still in me, by fits and starts'. The photographs are, he writes, 'the figurations of the body's prehistory' as it makes its way 'toward the labour and the pleasure of writing'. The images, Barthes writes, constitute the narrative (which 'ends with the subject's youth'): the written part of the autobiography (or, more accurately, anti-autobiography) is composed of textual fragments, which turn their back not only on chronology but on authorial identity.

Russian Album, the Canadian writer and politician Michael Ignatieff's account of his grandparents' lives (which were, like that of Vladimir Nabokov, split between pre-revolutionary Russia and post-revolutionary exile) opens with a different form of meditation on photograph, memory, identity, and history. Ignatieff suggests that: 'For many families, photographs are often the only artefacts to survive the passage through exile, migration or the pawnshop'. He notes the importance of photography 'as a new source of consciousness about the family past', which has also had a shaping effect on notions of personal identity: 'Because they bring us face to face with an inheritance that cannot be altered, photographs pose the problem of freedom: they seem to set the limits within which the self can be created.' In revealing characteristics that we have inherited from our ancestors, they seem to limit our capacity for self-invention.

Ignatieff also considers the relationship between photography and memory. 'Photographs', he writes, 'are the freeze frames that remind us how discontinuous our lives actually are.' By contrast, it is in 'a tight weave of forgetting and selective remembering that a continual self is knitted together'. Photographs are not adequate, he suggests, to a living history: 'photographs only document the distance that time has travelled; they cannot bind past and present together with meaning'. Ignatieff takes up some of the arguments of early 20th-century theorists of photography: 'Photography stops time and serves it back to us in disjunctive fragments. Memory integrates the visual within a weave of myth...Memory heals the scars of time. Photography documents the wounds.'

Photographs may bring back the past or they may stand in for, and hence replace, memory images. Is it events, places, and people that we recall, or photographs of them, in addition to the stories we are told about the past which we adopt as our own memories? Michael Baxendall writes in *Episodes* of the fragmentary (and photograph-like) quality of his memories of childhood which he sees as bound together by more mediated 'knowledge' of the past: 'These momentary glimpses, almost static snapshots, are linked into a story by rather thinner stuff—inference within bounds, knowledge of terrain and period props, authentic matter of memory but possibly supplied or supported from some more general stock'. As Freud wrote: 'Our childhood memories show us our earliest years not as they were but as they appeared at the later periods when the memories were aroused'.

Public figures aside, childhood is likely to have been the period when an individual is most fully photographed. The adult autobiographer's relationship to these images of a childhood self may reinforce the sense of childhood as a lost world, distinct, and separate from everything that came after it. There would seem to be significant connections not only between photography and autobiography in general but also between the advent of photography and the autobiography of childhood, which intensified throughout the 19th century and beyond.

The relationship between the photographic image and the memory image was explored in depth by the German critical theorist Siegfried Kracauer. In a 1927 essay, 'Photography', Kracauer argued that 'memory images are at odds with photographic representation', because photography 'grasps what is given as a spatial or temporal continuum' while 'memory's records are full of gaps'. 'An individual', he writes, 'retains memories because they are personally significant', though there is a 'truth' to the authentic memory image which transcends individual circumstance. 'In a photograph', by contrast, 'a person's history is buried as if under a layer of snow'.

Vladimir Nabokov's *Speak, Memory: An Autobiography Revisited* (1966) also opens up these questions in significant ways. Nabokov seems to echo Kracauer's understanding of memories as 'monograms'—a kind of personal insignia—when he writes of his search for 'the exact instrument that fashioned me, the anonymous roller that pressed upon my life a certain intricate watermark whose unique design becomes visible when the lamp of art is made to shine through life's foolscap' and whose tracing, in the form of 'thematic designs through one's life should be, I think, the true purpose of autobiography'.

Nabokov uses metaphors of photography, and other visual technologies, to explore the workings of memory: 'In probing my childhood...I see the awakening of consciousness as a series of spaced flashes, with the intervals between them gradually diminishing until bright blocks of perception are formed, according memory a slippery hold'. Scenes and images from childhood appear like early photographic 'transparencies' or 'decalcomania pictures'. 'I am going to show a few slides', Nabokov writes, in describing his childhood tutors, whose images appear 'within memory's luminous disc as so many magic-lantern projections'.

It may seem paradoxical that he recalls an unloved tutor's actual 'Educational Magic-Lantern Projections' as episodes of squirming embarrassment, but it is in fact at one with the ways in which Nabokov seeks to be his own projector and instrument of vision, and not a passive receiver of 'views'. The tutor's lantern-slides are 'tawdry and tumid' when projected on the 'damp linen screen', but 'what loveliness the glass slides as such revealed when simply held between finger and thumb and raised to the light—translucent miniatures, pocket wonderlands, neat little worlds of hushed luminous hues!' Photographic images do not replace memory images for Nabokov; memory, rather, puts photography (and other optics) into its own service. Coloured panes of glass on the veranda are 'magic glasses': 'of all the windows this is the pane through which in later years parched nostalgia longed to peer'. Memory and vision are inseparable from the autobiography's abiding themes of loss and exile—the Nabokov family fled Russia in 1919—both from the past and from place.

Writing about photography is frequently tinged by the melancholic and the elegiac. As Susan Sontag writes, in *On Photography*: 'All photographs are *memento mori*... Precisely by slicing out this moment and freezing it, all photographs testify to time's relentless melt.' For Roland Barthes, the tense of the photograph is 'That-has-been': 'it has been here, and yet immediately separated; it has been absolutely, irrefutably present, and yet already deferred'. He wrote these words in his book on photography, *La Chambre claire*, which is also a work of mourning: in particular, for his deceased mother, a photograph of whom—the 'Winter Garden Photograph'—he talks about but does not reproduce for the reader: 'It exists only for me'.

For other writers, the work of photography and of memory is to bring, in the film and cultural theorist Annette Kuhn's words, 'the secrets and shadows into the open': 'the past is like the scene of a crime: if the deed itself is irrecoverable, its traces may still remain'. Kuhn's *Family Secrets* is a series of essays revolving around photographs (in particular, family photographs, including images of herself as a child), film, and 'the stories we tell about the past'. She defines her writing as neither autobiography (understood, in rather conventional terms, by Kuhn as a 'life story organized as a linear narrative with a beginning, a middle and an end, in that order') nor confession, but as 'memory-work' and 'memory-text', and photographs are at the heart of this task.

The photograph in autobiography

While autobiographers frequently attach captions, and sometimes comments, to photographs (Nabokov's are particularly detailed), there is often little or no commentary on these images in the body of the text. There are, however, a number of autobiographies in which photographs do not appear merely as unremarked or seemingly incidental illustrations but become central to the narration. J. R. Ackerley's *My Father and Myself*, with its sleuthing into family secrets and its openness about its author's homosexuality, incorporates photographs of his father, Roger Ackerley, as a young guardsman and with a group of male companions. He was, J. R. Ackerley writes, 'a mystery man'. It is with the discovery of the photographs that 'the inherent absurdity of envisaging my father in the arms of another man […] faded […] What irony if it could be proved that he had led in this youth the very kind of life that I was leading!' The aspect of the photograph which is both fascinating and disquieting for the autobiographer is that it can represent a world and a time prior to his or her birth, opening on to a past in which he or she is not yet present.

For some autobiographers, photographs indeed seem nearer to 'proof' than memory or the written word, and though their truth is by no means absolute or, at least, is reliant on interpretation, their very distortions can be revealing. Paul Auster's *The Invention of Solitude* describes a number of family photographs, but includes only two as actual images. It has, as its front cover, a trick 'multiplicity photograph' of his evasive and emotionally absent father, whose multiplied image seems to embody the disappearing act which was his life: 'It is a picture of death, a portrait of an invisible man' (see Figure 6). The silence surrounding a scandal in the family appears in visual form through a torn and patched-together photograph, from which the figure of his grandfather has been cut out, so that only his fingertips remain. The torn photograph becomes an image not only of family secrets but also of the 'wound' Auster experiences in relation to his father's death—and his life. The American author Susan Faludi's memoir *In the Darkroom* uses her father's professional work as a 'trick photographer'—'dodging' (making dark areas look light), 'masking' (concealing unwanted parts of the picture), and making a perfect copy from a print—as a metaphor for the secrets, evasions, and assumed identities by and through which he lived: 'He made the story come out the way he wanted it to'.

In a number of recent autobiographical, or semi-autobiographical works, photographs float more freely and enigmatically within the

6. Paul Auster, 'multiplicity photograph' of his father, 'Portrait of an Invisible Man', in *The Invention of Solitude*.

written text, unmoored by captions. This is central to the work of W. G. Sebald, a number of whose texts, including *The Rings of Saturn*, intertwine life-writing and fiction. Some of the photographs Sebald includes would seem to be postcard images; generic views, which we perceive as detached from any individual photographer's vision. Personal memory and cultural memory are intertwined.

The Turkish novelist Orhan Pamuk's *Istanbul: Memories and the City*, which is both a memoir of childhood and a guide to the city, is also structured around photographs, which are not captioned but work to interweave writing, visual image, and memory image. Like Sebald, Pamuk includes only black-and-white photographs, representing a city that is, he writes, for its inhabitants, experienced in black and white: 'To see the city in black and white is to see it through the tarnish of history: the patina of what is old and faded and no longer matters to the rest of the world'. Black and white is also the medium of memory, in its many layers, from the photographs through which, as a child, Pamuk constituted his family history and his own place within it, to the 'old black-and-white films' representing Istanbul and its 'broken-down mansions in black and white' that he now watches. In viewing these, 'I sometimes forget I am watching a film; stupefied by melancholy, I sometimes feel as if I am watching my own past'.

Pamuk links photography and film, rather than (as have some critics) separating them along the lines of time/memory as stasis and time/memory as flow. There has been less exploration of autobiography in relation to film and video than to other visual media, but in recent years there has been an increasing interest in the 'autobiographical film'. This is not only a matter of a cinematic representation of a life-story (an 'autobiopic', to coin a term) but also of experiments with the representation of the world, and at times the part-self, as perceived and captured by the eye (as an equivalent to the autobiographer's 'I') behind the camera.

The French artist and writer Sophie Calle, to take one example, has worked with both photography and film to record the narrative events, encounters, and pursuits which she has constructed and staged in various cities: she has been described as a 'first-person artist'. Her projects with Paul Auster have arisen from their shared absorption in chance and contingency, particularly as they relate to urban life. They reveal the legacies of the early 20th-century surrealist fascination with the question of what is random and what is given in the experiences that make up our lives, and with the erotic potential of the chance meeting. André Breton's *Nadja* is a central work here: its first words trouble autobiographical identity ('Who am I? If this once I were to rely on a proverb, then perhaps everything would amount to knowing whom I "haunt"') and it is an early example of writing in which photographs 'haunt' the text.

Autobiography as performance

Recent theoretical approaches to questions of identity and selfhood have included a focus on 'self-fashioning' (Stephen Greenblatt's term for the processes by which 'Renaissance man' modelled his identity and public persona in accord with established cultural norms and role models) and 'performativity'. In these models, the self is not 'given' but 'made'. 'Performativity' was most influentially explored in the work of the cultural and gender theorist Judith Butler. Butler argued, in her book *Gender Trouble*, for a shift from a 'grammar of identity' (that is, 'being' male or female) to an account of 'doing gender' as a performative enactment. (Her theories follow on from the philosopher J. L. Austin's work on 'performative utterances'—such as 'I now declare you man and wife'—in which the word and what it 'performs' are one.) The 'performance' of gender must be reiterated at each and every moment so that it can appear to be fixed and stable. The 'performative' and 'performance' thus become closely related terms.

In the history of autobiography, the act of self-presentation may conjure up theatrical performance as well as visual self-representation and self-display. The self may appear, metaphorically, in many costumes and guises. The large body of autobiographical writing produced, across the centuries, by actors and actresses reveals a history of 'celebrity' as well as a very particular version of the 'double consciousness' (in this case, the acting self and the private self) associated with the autobiographical act more generally.

'Performance' is also at the heart of the projects of self-representation that have become increasingly prevalent in the visual arts. The major work of the young artist Charlotte Salomon, born in Berlin in 1917 and murdered in Auschwitz in 1943, is titled *Life? Or Theatre? A Play with Music* (see Figure 7). *Life? Or Theatre?* consists of more than 800 gouache paintings narrating, through both image and word, the story of Salomon's life, including her troubled family history and the times through which she lived.

The early decades of the 20th century also saw forms of photographic self-staging, as in the work of the artist-photographers Man Ray and Claude Cahun, both of whom played with gender identities and cross-gendered roles. Such representations of the self as other, and as its other, have been revisited in the work of contemporary artists including Gillian Wearing (who, like Cahun, is fascinated by masks and identities), Cindy Sherman (best known for her photographic self-portraits in the guise of film stars and, more contentiously, murder victims), and ORLAN (who photographs the bodily mutations she has undergone through plastic surgery). The self and the body are the materials with and on which these artists work, but they reject models of stable identity. Instead, they enact and represent the creation of multiple selves, projects of self-transformation, and the changes to appearance wrought by the passing of time.

7. Charlotte Salomon, final painting in *Life? Or Theatre?* series.

In recent years the 'selfie' has transformed photographic
self-portraiture and the 'selfie stick' enables the insertion of the
photographer into a larger scene. The term selfie seems to have
emerged in Australia around the beginning of the present century,
and the practice took off with the arrival of the camera phone
in 2003 and the concurrent explosion of social media such as
Facebook. Smartphones allow us simultaneously to see and

record ourselves, combining mirror and camera. Like other forms of self-representation, selfies have been seen as narcissistic or 'oversharing', though some studies have suggested that they should be seen as a normal part of modern life for many people, like the photograph which one expects to find on a person's website. As Jill Walker Rettberg concludes her recent book, *Seeing Ourselves Through Technology*, 'We no longer need to rely on others to represent us. We represent ourselves.'

Chapter 8
Autobiographies, autobiographical novels, and autofictions

It has been a widely held view that the genre of autobiography did not flourish among the literary modernists of the early 20th century, with few of the great modernist writers producing explicit or fully fledged autobiographies. Such an assumption has shifted in recent years, not least as the category of autobiography has become more expansive, with the term 'life-writing' taking in a range of personal writings. The publication of extensive, and often complete, editions of the letters and diaries of a number of modernist writers, including James Joyce, Virginia Woolf, and Katherine Mansfield, and more recently W. B. Yeats, T. S. Eliot, and Samuel Beckett, has contributed to a new, or renewed, focus on the person of the author as well as the processes and stages of literary creation.

Letters, journals, and diaries as genres may differ in structure from 'autobiography', frequently defined as a retrospective form, but they nonetheless make up a central part of what we understand to be autobiographical writing. Autobiographers frequently turn to their letters and diaries in composing their accounts of the past, using them as evidence of what they once thought and felt. In the present time of their writing, diaries and journals can function as a form of self-analysis or dialogue with the self, in the French tradition of the *journal intime*.

When published, usually posthumously, they can represent a very charged and intense relationship to living, as in the cases of the journals of Marie Bashkirtseff (who died in Paris of consumption at the age of twenty-four, and who became a crucial figure for Katherine Mansfield in her late teens) and W. N. P. Barbellion's *The Journal of a Disappointed Man*, the diary of a young, self-educated naturalist with a terminal illness, which was an extraordinary success on its publication in 1919.

The expansion of the 'life-writing' category has also made visible the prevalence of autobiographical novels and *romans à clef* in the period, including works by Mansfield, James Joyce, D. H. Lawrence, Dorothy Richardson, and Virginia Woolf. It has revealed the extent to which fiction entered the autobiographical terrain in the late 19th and early 20th centuries. This was part of an increasingly 'aesthetic' approach to autobiography, but it also showed a growing scepticism about autobiography's powers to represent the self and to recapture the past. New genres arose which blended life-writing and fiction, such as the personal essay, the 'imaginary portrait', and novels which incorporated authentic letters and journal entries. As Max Saunders has shown, the coining of the term 'autobiografiction' by the writer Stephen Reynolds, in an article published in 1906, indicates the centrality of a mode of writing at the turn of the century in which fact and fiction merge.

In Reynolds's definition, 'autobiografiction is a record of real spiritual experiences strung on a credible but more or less fictitious autobiographical narrative'. The 'fictitious' dimension might include attributing autobiographical experiences to a fictional character. Reynolds's examples included works by Mark Rutherford (the pen name of William Hale White, who wrote an autobiography in Rutherford's name and whose *The House of Quiet* takes the form of a dead man's journal), George Gissing, and A. C. Benson. It also looks back to Thomas Carlyle's mock-autobiography *Sartor Resartus* and Charles Lamb's *The Essays of Elia*.

For many late 19th- and early 20th-century writers, the 'self' was perceived as a fiction or a mask. Complex understandings of the nature of self and identity, influenced by early 20th-century philosophies and by psychoanalysis, led to the view that conventional forms of autobiography were not adequate to the multiplicity of selves that make up the single individual. The self was understood to have substrates which were not knowable and communicable in any direct way. Autobiographical fiction, with its possibilities for multiple perspectives on characters and situations, answered to the need to represent complex, composite, and divided selves, creating the most appropriate vehicles for identities which can never be fully known.

Competing models of the self as many-faceted or as a single unity, discussed in Chapter 4, were explored in lectures given by the French philosopher Henri Bergson in the early 1910s. He took the topic back to the ancient Greek philosopher Plotinus, for whom, in Bergson's words, the central issue is: 'How can our person be on the one hand single, on the other hand multiple?' Plotinus' answer was, Bergson wrote, that 'each of us was multiple "in our lower nature" and single "in our higher nature"'. Bergson does not embrace this hierarchy, but it can be glimpsed in Katherine Mansfield's image of the self as a plant which grows through years of darkness and is finally discovered by the light: 'and—we are alive—we are flowering for our moment upon the earth? This is the moment which, after all, we live for—the moment of direct feeling when we are most ourselves and least personal.'

The paradox that 'we are most ourselves' when 'least personal' connects to one of the central issues in modernist literature: the topic of 'impersonality'. Mansfield wrote in her journal for January 1920 that her 'philosophy' was 'the defeat of the personal', an assertion linked to T. S. Eliot's proclamation, in his essay 'Tradition and the Individual Talent', that: 'The progress of an artist is a continual self-sacrifice, a continual extinction of personality' and that the poet has 'not a "personality" to express but a particular medium'. The authority of Eliot's statements on this topic has been largely responsible for the perception of modernism as an anti-autobiographical movement. Yet critics in recent decades have pointed up the complexities and inconsistencies in the modernist doctrine of 'impersonality' (including Eliot's own claim that one must have a 'personality' in order to wish to escape it), and have suggested that it proved a spur rather than a barrier to experiments in life-writing.

Distancing and displacement are defining features of much modernist autobiographical experimentation, from the autobiographical novel, the Bildungsroman and Künstlerroman (the story of the making of the artist) and the *roman à clef* through to third-person autobiographies, including Gertrude Stein's *The Autobiography of Alice B. Toklas*, in which Stein writes her own life as if in the voice of Alice, her life-partner. A number of modernist writers shared the perception that the truest autobiography would emerge in fictional form. D. H. Lawrence expressed deep resistance to writing a direct account of his life—'I simply can't write biographies of myself'—and prefaced an autobiographical account, entitled 'Mushrooms', of which we have only a fragment, with this disclaimer:

> It is perhaps absurd for any man to write his own autobiography. The one person I find it impossible to 'know' is myself. I have dozens of little pictures of what purports to be myself, and which is me? None of them. The little animal is now a bigger animal. But which sort of animal it is, I do not know, and do not vastly care.

When pressed for a written account of himself by the writer and editor Philippe Soupault, Lawrence wrote: 'With great reluctance I have forced myself to write out a draft of an autobiography—Let [Soupault] read *Sons and Lovers* and *The Rainbow*—and he's got all he wants.' His assertion that *Sons and Lovers* was 'all autobiography' implies both that it is in the fiction that the truth is to be had and that a writer's truest autobiography lies in his fictional works. Yet it should be noted that there are only partial correspondences between life-events and the narratives of Lawrence's early novels and that he wrote and rewrote the materials of his first fictions, altering them in response, for example, to the knowledge he had gained of Freud's theories, which shaped his representations of Paul Morel's love for his mother and hatred of his father in *Sons and Lovers*.

While creating a fictional narrative from aspects of his experience, Lawrence was also able, through the use of the novel form, to represent events and experiences which lay outside his own memory and consciousness: those, in particular, relating to his parents before his birth. Lawrence was by no means alone among writers in seeking, through the medium of autobiographical fiction, to infer or imagine a past which did not yet contain him, but which would, quite literally, bring him into being.

In the thirteen volumes of *Pilgrimage*, written between 1915 and 1946, Dorothy Richardson charted the experiences of the years between 1891 and 1912 through the consciousness of her fictional alter-ego, Miriam Henderson. H. G. Wells (whose fictional counterpart in the novel-sequence is the character Hypo Wilson) described the *Pilgrimage* volumes as 'a very curious essay in autobiography'. *Pilgrimage* troubles generic categories. It is an autobiographical fiction, a quest sequence and a journey, and a woman's Bildungsroman or Künstlerroman: in the final volumes of the sequence we see Miriam begin to write her story. Written substantially in the third person, though at times moving into first-person narration, *Pilgrimage* creates a new literary space between the genres of autobiography and the novel.

In an autobiographical sketch, *Beginnings*, Richardson noted the ways in which experience and thought bring into being 'the divided mind'. 'Instruction and experience', she writes, inevitably shape the mind which comes to observe the past, 'befogging' and destroying what was once known and felt. Many modernist texts attempt to go behind or before such mediations and to recapture those perceptions and understandings that held sway (most powerfully in the child's mind) before their inevitable effacement.

Woolf wrote the fullest of her directly autobiographical works in the final years of her life, turning to the memoir that would become *Sketch of the Past* in 1939, as she worked on her biography of Roger Fry. Earlier autobiographical sketches, such as 'Hyde Park Gate', were produced in the context of the Bloomsbury Group's 'Memoir Club', a gathering in which the group's members would take it in turns to deliver autobiographical accounts of their lives and experiences. Woolf and her peers both produced and commented extensively on the genres of biography and autobiography. Writing of the overwhelmingly male canon of autobiographical writing, Woolf noted that there had been no woman's autobiography to rival Rousseau's *Confessions*: 'Chastity and modesty have I suppose been the reason'.

The failure of so many autobiographies, Woolf writes, is that they 'leave out the person to whom things happened'. The interest of autobiography, she suggests, lies not in events but in identities, and a central difficulty of the genre relates not only to self-knowledge but to knowledge of those other minds by which the self can measure its likeness and its difference. The central problem of autobiography, Woolf argues, is the nature of time: 'for no sooner has one said this was so, then it was past and altered'. The perception, which takes us back to the classical philosopher Heraclitus ('one cannot step into the same river twice'), is also a modernist one, in its apprehension of the fleeting, evanescent, and fluid qualities of identity and experience: an apprehension which lies at the heart of modernist autobiography.

The perception that the borders between fiction and autobiography are porous became prominent in autobiography in the course of the 20th century. 'It must all be considered as if spoken by a character in a novel', was Barthes's opening epigraph in his autobiography, *Roland Barthes by Roland Barthes*. His view is connected to the idea that what makes us human is our capacity for storytelling. For a number of narrative theorists, it is said to be the act of narrating, and the absorbing of the narratives of others, that enables us to deal with what shapes our human lives—time, destiny, mortality—and to create and project our identities, ourselves, in a world of other individuals. The philosopher Paul Ricœur, author of the three-volume study *Time and Narrative*, wrote of autobiography that: 'the story of a life continues to be refigured by all the truthful or fictive stories a subject tells about himself or herself. This refiguration makes life itself a cloth woven of stories told.'

Recent work in cognitive narrative theory has suggested that narrative is fundamental to cognition and thought; we are meaning-making creatures, and the ways in which we make meaning is by telling stories about our perceptual world. For V. S. Naipaul, writing in his autobiographical work *Finding the Centre*: 'I also live, as it were, in a novel of my own making, moving from not knowing to knowing, with person interweaving with person and incident opening out to incident.'

Autofiction

Serge Doubrovsky, one of the leading French writers on 'autofiction', has argued that since the 1980s the novel has been eclipsed by the autobiographical narrative, reversing the earlier sense that autobiographical writing was of secondary importance. He coined the term 'autofiction' in 1977 in his autobiographical novel *Fils* (the title referring both to the strings of a kite and to the son, Doubrovsky himself). It has been variously defined, from a minimalist form in which it stresses the reimagined quality of the life to a stronger version in which the life serves as the basis for an essentially novelistic product, inventing scenes which may not have had any basis in reality. Authors writing in this genre have welcomed the freedom it affords them, for example in writing about others in a way which protects their privacy—something stressed by Doubrovsky's compatriot Annie Ernaux in relation to her confessional writings.

Philippe Lejeune, the doyen of autobiographical theory, responded to autofiction in his book *Moi aussi*. He had defined autobiography in 1975 as a 'retrospective narrative in prose that a real person makes of his own life when putting emphasis on his/her personal life, especially on the history of his/her personality', stressing what he called the 'autobiographical pact' between writer and reader; that the writer is the person described and that what is described really happened. He was therefore particularly struck by Doubrovsky's use of his own name in what he presented as a novel. Doubrovsky claimed in a letter to Lejeune that he had deliberately done this as he finished his book in order to fill in an empty box in Lejeune's table of autobiographical modes: it was a combination which Lejeune had described as possible but so far not instantiated.

Lejeune stresses the influence on Doubrovsky of the *nouveau roman* (the experimental 'new novel' of the 1950s and 1960s in France) and assigns him to the class of novelists and not of autobiographers such as Michel Leiris, with his 'ethical concern for truth'. Perhaps, he suggests, 'autofiction is a homage to truth paid by the lie'. Sylvie Coster, another writer of a novel taken to be autobiographical, declared in an interview that the sad parts were true and the funny parts invented. 'It's not a real autobiography because there are times when you get bored writing just about what happened. You escape a little bit, you put in some things which didn't happen.'

The Norwegian writer Karl Ove Knausgaard's six-volume work, *Min Kamp* (provocatively taking the title of Hitler's autobiography *Mein Kampf*), translated into English as *My Struggle*, also tests the boundaries of genre. The volumes have been classified by their publishers as 'fiction', and on occasion as the 'non-fiction novel', but a substantial part of their interest lies in the fact that the events described have almost certainly been lived rather than imagined. Knausgaard uses his own name, as well as the real names of many of his family and friends, throughout *My Struggle*, and names become important markers of identity: the 'autobiographical pact' is enacted in explicit ways.

'Writing is recalling', Knausgaard has stated in interview: 'I think that all our ages, all our experiences are kept in us, all we need is a reminder of something, and then something else is released'. The volumes of the work recount experiences, emotions, and conversations, some from decades previously, in the most detailed ways, raising the question of how the past could conceivably be remembered so vividly and closely. There is undoubtedly a substantial element of constructed or invented detail in *My Struggle*. Yet the fact of invention seems secondary—even unimportant—by comparison with what Knausgaard has termed 'world-nearness' or 'proximity to the world', linked to the intensely visual quality of his acts of memory.

Knausgaard's life-narrative is not predominantly linear and chronological, unlike Dorothy Richardson's *Pilgrimage* (with which there are interesting connections, as there are with Proust's *À la recherche du temps perdu*, which Knausgaard describes himself as having 'imbibed'). The second volume of *My Struggle*, *A Man in Love*, for example, details a much later period of Knausgaard's life than the third, *Boyhood Island*. Within each volume, there will be movements away from the recounting of past presents, or the present time of writing, into either the remembered past or an already lived future, triggered by association and memory.

Such complex temporal structures notwithstanding, the overwhelming quality of the work is the experience of day-to-day, moment-by-moment, existence. In the first volume, *A Death in the Family*, Knausgaard and his brother, young men in their twenties, are staying in their aged and confused grandmother's house, in which their alcoholic father spent his last years and in which he has died. Over a hundred or so pages, Knausgaard describes the details of this time in suspension—the days between the discovery of the father's body and his funeral—including the work of cleaning the squalid house. This is 'everyday life' which is at once ordinary and overwhelming: the reader experiences viscerally not only the labour of the procedures but also the intensity of the emotions driving them.

In analysing the nature of *My Struggle*'s popular success, one commentator has suggested that, in an age of multi-tasking and limited attention spans, the work of entering another human being's consciousness through the act of reading—'dousing yourself daily in the discipline of a single, extended, difficult and deeply private work of art for weeks on end'—has profound rewards. Similar claims could, and have, been made for the processes of reading any substantial literary work: it performs the 'ethical' task of opening us up to thoughts, realities, and imaginings that are not our own; it demands our focus and attention. Yet there is, perhaps, perceived to be a particular quality to such immersion when the work that is absorbed has the qualities of 'real life'.

The other side of this perceived relationship between autobiography, or autofiction, and ethical responses is the breach of privacy entailed in the 'laying bare' of existence. Knausgaard's project has been placed in opposition to the 'multiple platforms and multiple subjects' of our mediated world. It could be argued, however, that it shares the anti-reticence of a culture in which it is the norm to put oneself (and those around one) on display. Certainly, a number of Knausgaard's relatives have expressed extreme discomfort with their representation in his work, and with the making public of private family matters.

Much recent writing which has blurred the boundaries between autobiography and fiction is characterized by such breaking of taboos around revealing the intimacies of private life. The avant-garde writer and art theorist Chris Kraus's *I Love Dick* first appeared in 1997 but found a much wider audience when it was republished in 2006; in 2017 it was adapted as a television series. As Kraus herself has written, the more welcoming reception of the book on republication registers the cultural changes, including a rejection of 'the unspoken rule of feminine discretion', that had occurred over a decade.

Of *I Love Dick*, Kraus has written: 'Everything that happens in it happened first in life, but that doesn't mean that it's a memoir'. While literary theorists have, over a number of decades, sought to define the precise properties of, and distinctions between, autobiography, memoir, autography, novel, and essay, the authors of many contemporary literary and cultural works are refusing to respect just such boundaries, often in the name of an avant-garde and 'performative' element to their work or with reference to the determining nature of its reception. 'What makes something fiction', Kraus writes, 'isn't whether it's true or not—it's whether it's bracketed in time, how it's treated and edited, and whether it's construed as a work of fiction'.

The Canadian writer Sheila Heti has named *I Love Dick* as a particular inspiration for her best-known work, *How Should a Person Be?* (2010). The letters of Kraus's 1996 text become the emails of Heti's 2010 work, which also includes lengthy sections of transcribed conversations and recorded interviews between 'Sheila' and her group of friends, suggestive of 'reality T.V.' Asked in an interview about the difference between herself and her 'alter-ego Sheila', Heti answered that: 'Writing, for me, when I'm writing in the first-person, is like a form of acting. So as I'm writing, the character or self I'm writing about and my whole self—when I began the book—become entwined...But that voice or character comes out of a part of me that exists already.' On completion of the book, she adds, that self falls away, but 'a different self from the original one is left'. Her account of this process emphasizes the performative nature both of writing and identity, as well as the (now familiar) idea that what we call the self is in fact composed of multiple selves. Finally, the processes of putting these selves into writing entails an alteration to what might be thought of as that 'original self' which both preceded and initiated the written work.

Works such as Kraus's and Heti's point to important transformations in autobiographical writing. The uses of 'I' and of the 'proper name' which connects author with narrator are accompanied by a desire to produce works which are collective and communal in origin, as the texts gather up the letters, emails, and recorded words of others. There is a refusal of the concept of 'confessional' writing, but an equal distancing from fiction-making: 'Increasingly, I'm less interested in writing about fictional people because it seems so tiresome to make up a fake person and put them through the paces of a fake story. I just—I can't do it', Heti told an interviewer in 2007.

Such views do not represent those of all contemporary authors. Elena Ferrante's quartet of Neapolitan novels has been an extraordinary success in recent years, absorbing readers in ways similar to Knausgaard's *My Struggle*, but authorship has worked very differently in the two cases. Ferrante is the pseudonym of a writer who has resolutely preserved her (or, conceivably, his) anonymity. While critics have pointed to 'the intensely, violently personal' nature of the works, Ferrante, in written interview, has stated: 'If I had wanted to recount my own business, I would have established a different pact with the reader, I would have signalled I was writing an autobiography. I have not chosen an autobiographical path, nor will I choose it in the future, because I am convinced that fiction, when it works, is more charged with truth.'

Other writers are rejecting distinctions between the literatures of 'truth' and those of 'invention'. The American novelist Nicole Krauss writes, with reference to her novel *Forest Dark*, that the choice of the name Nicole for her central character 'felt authentic to me':

> In a sense, the self is more or less an invention from beginning to end...Why do we have such a heavy investment in knowing what is true and what isn't true about people's lives? Why is it even valid to make a distinction between autobiography, auto-fiction and fiction itself? What fiction doesn't contain a deep reflection of the author's perspective and memory and sense of the world?

This view takes us back to Nietzsche's assertion of the autobiographical basis of all philosophy, and to claims made by many writers, among them Jean Cocteau and J. M. Coetzee, that 'all writing is autobiography'.

On the question of autobiographical truth, we might turn to the words of the 19th-century American writer Mark Twain: 'An autobiography is the truest of all books; for while it inevitably consists mainly of extinctions of the truth, shirkings of the truth, partial revealments of the truth, with hardly an instance of plain straight truth, the remorseless truth is there, between the lines...the result being that the reader knows the author in spite of his wily diligences'. The provocative autobiographies and autofictions of the present day undoubtedly have a different relationship to concealment and revelation: there is very much less that must be disguised and hidden, and few taboos that cannot be broken. Nonetheless, questions of 'truth', 'reality', and 'world-nearness', whether or not they are contrasted with 'fiction-making', are topics to which writers, critics, and readers return, ensuring that 'autobiography' continues to be not merely one genre among others, but a nodal point for perennial questions posed in literature and in life.

References

Introduction

Philippe Lejeune, *Le Pacte autobiographique* (Paris: Seuil, 1975), 14. See also Lejeune, *L'Autobiographie en France* (Paris: A. Colin, 1971).

William Wordsworth, *The Prelude 1799, 1805, 1850*, ed. Jonathan Wordsworth, M. H. Abrams, and Stephen Gill (New York: Norton, 1993).

Paul de Man, 'Autobiography as De-Facement', *Modern Language Notes*, 94 (1979), 919–30.

William James, *Principles of Psychology* (New York: Dover, 2015), vol. 1, 294.

M. K. Gandhi, *An Autobiography* (London: Penguin, 2001), 14. My book focuses mainly on European and North American autobiography, but there are also of course rich traditions in China, Japan, Iran, Tibet, and elsewhere.

John Stuart Mill, *Collected Works of John Stuart Mill*, ed. John M. Robson and Jack Stillinger (Indianapolis: Liberty Fund, 2006), vol. 1; 5.

Harriet Martineau, *Harriet Martineau's Autobiography* (London: Virago, 1983 [1877]), 1; 4.

Charles Darwin, *Autobiography* (London: Collins, 1887), 21; 27.

G. Thomas Couser, *Memoir. An Introduction* (New York: Oxford University Press, 2012), esp. 18.

Ben Yagoda, *Memoir: A History* (New York: Riverhead, 2009).

William Gass, 'The Art of Self: Autobiography in an Age of Narcissism', *Harper's Magazine* (May 1994), 48.

Chapter 1: Confession, conversion, testimony

Virginia Woolf, 'Sketch of the Past', in *Moments of Being: Unpublished Autobiographical Writings*, ed. Jeanne Schulkind (New York: Harcourt Brace Jovanovich, 1976), 75.

Michel Foucault, *Histoire de la sexualité 1* (Paris: Gallimard, 1984).

Peter Brooks, *Troubling Confessions: Speaking Guilt in Law and Literature* (Chicago: University of Chicago Press, 2000), 6; 102.

Augustine, *Confessions*, tr. R. S. Pine-Coffin (Harmondsworth: Penguin, 1961), 177–8; 91; 207; 170; 216; 206; 208.

On the notion of the turning-point, see Michael Sheringham, 'Conversion and Turning-Points', in Margaretta Jolly (ed.), *Encyclopedia of Life Writing* (London: Fitzroy Dearborn, 2001), 232–4.

Julian of Norwich, *Revelations of Divine Love*, tr. Barry Windeatt (Oxford: Oxford University Press, 2015); see Nancy Bradley Warren, 'Incarnational (Auto)biography', in Paul Strohm (ed.), *Middle English* (Oxford: Oxford University Press, 2007), 369–85.

La vida de la Santa Madre Teresa de Jesús, y algunas de las mercedes que Dios le hizo, escritas por ella misma (The Life of Saint Teresa of Ávila...Written by Herself) (Madrid: M. Rivadeneyra, 1861), 41. <http://www.cervantesvirtual.com/obra/la-vida-de-la-santa-madre-teresa-de-jesus-y-algunas-de-las-mercedes-que-dios-le-hizo-escritas-por-ella-misma--0/>. Accessed 16 December 2017.

The Book of Margery Kempe, tr. Anthony Bale (Oxford: Oxford University Press, 2015).

James Fraser, *Memoirs of the Life of the Very Reverend Mr James Fraser, of Brea: Written by Himself* (Glasgow: Printed by Joseph Galbraith, for Alexander M'Kenzie, the publisher, 2nd edition, 1798), 84.

On the centrality of 'imitation' in spiritual writings, see in the early 15th century the *Imitation of Christ* (attributed to Thomas à Kempis), itself a much imitated work.

Jean-Jacques Rousseau, *Les Confessions* (Paris: Launette, 1889), 1; 80–2; 11; 26; 47.

George Henry Lewes, 'Recent Novels: French and English', *Fraser's Magazine* 36 (1847), 686–95.

John Bunyan, *Grace Abounding: With Other Spiritual Autobiographies*, ed. John Stachniewski and Anita Pacheo (Oxford: Oxford University Press, 1998).

John Henry Cardinal Newman, *Apologia Pro Vita Sua*, ed. A. Dwight Culler (Boston: Riverside Press, 1956), 3; 227.

Thomas De Quincey, *Confessions of an English Opium-Eater and Other Writings*, ed. Grevel Lindop (Oxford: Oxford University Press, 1985), 2; 92.

Oscar Wilde, 'The Critic as Artist', in *The Works of Oscar Wilde 1856–1900*, ed. G. F. Maine (London and Glasgow: Collins, 1948), 50.

Wilde, *De Profundis* (London: Methuen, 1949), 50.

Wilde, *De Profundis*, 31; 59.

De Quincey, *Confessions*, 69.

Benjamin Franklin, *The Autobiography* (New York: New American Library, 1961), 28; 4; 60.

De Quincey, *Confessions*, 78; 61.

Václav Havel, *Open Letters: Selected Writings, 1965–1990* (London: Faber, 1991).

Malcolm X, with the assistance of Alex Haley, *The Autobiography of Malcolm X* (London: Penguin, 2007).

Andrew O'Hagan, 'Ghosting', *London Review of Books*, 36(5) (6 March 2014), 5–26.

J. M. Coetzee, *Giving Offense: Essays on Censorship* (Chicago: University of Chicago Press, 1996), 164.

J. M. Coetzee, *Boyhood: Scenes from Provincial Life* (New York: Vintage, 1998), 119.

Frederick Douglass, *Narrative of the Life of Frederick Douglass, an American Slave* (New York: Penguin, 1982), 78.

Harriet Jacobs, *Incidents in the Life of a Slave Girl* (New York: Signet, 2010), 109.

Vera Brittain, *Testament of Youth* (New York: Macmillan, 1933).

Primo Levi, *If This Is a Man* (1958), tr. Stuart Woolf (London: Abacus, 1987), 15; 47.

Otto Dov Kulka, *Landscapes of the Metropolis of Death*, tr. Ralph Mandel (London: Allen Lane, 2013), 9.

Stefan Maechler, *The Wilkomirski Affair: A Study in Biographical Truth*, tr. John E. Woods (London: Picador, 2001), 271.

The Prelude, Book 11, 411: line 372.

The Prelude, Book 7, 251: lines 461–5.

The Prelude, Book 2, 67: lines 31–3.

The Prelude, Book 2, 85: lines 346; 358.

The Prelude, Book 2, 77: lines 228–32.

Jean-Jacques Rousseau, *Les Rêveries du promeneur solitaire* (Paris: Gallimard, 1965), 122.

Ralph Waldo Emerson, *Nature and Selected Essays* (New York: Penguin, 1982), 39.

William Wordsworth, *The Excursion*, in *The Complete Poetical Works*, with an introduction by John Morley (London: Macmillan and Co., 1888), 1–2.

Ralph Waldo Emerson, Introduction to Henry Thoreau, *Walden and Other Writings* (New York: Modern Library, 2000), xviii.

Thoreau, *Walden and Other Writings*, 3; 86; 631; 16; 68; 166; 169; 176; 269–70; 182; 189.

Benjamin Franklin, *The Autobiography* (New York: New American Library, 1961), 4.

Walt Whitman, *Leaves of Grass*, edited with an Introduction and Notes by Jerome Loving (New York: Oxford University Press, 1998).

Robert F. Sayre, *New Essays on Walden* (New York: Cambridge University Press, 2008), 24.

Alfred Kazin, *A Walker in the City* (Orlando: Harcourt, 1951), 99; 21–2; 172; 52.

Rebecca Solnit, *A Book of Migrations* (London: Verso, 2011), 82; xii.

Jan Morris, *Conundrum* (London: Faber and Faber, 2002).

Iain Sinclair, *Guardian* interview, 2004, cited in Merlin Coveley, *Psychogeography* (Harpenden: Pocket Essentials, 2006), 122.

Chapter 3: Autobiographical consciousness

R. G. Collingwood, *An Autobiography and Other Writings, with essays on Collingwood's life and work*, ed. David Boucher and Teresa Smith (Oxford: Oxford University Press, 2013), xxxvi. See also Thomas Mathien and D. G. Wright (eds), *Autobiography as Philosophy: The Philosophical Uses of Self-Presentation* (London: Routledge, 2006).

John Locke, *An Essay Concerning Human Understanding*, ed. A. D. Woozley (Glasgow: Collins, 1977), 212.

A. Kenny, 1966, 'Cartesian Privacy', in G. Pitcher (ed.), *Wittgenstein: The Philosophical Investigations* (London: Macmillan, 1968).

A. J. Ayer, *Part of My Life* (London: Collins, 1977), 220.

Stanley Cavell, *A Pitch of Philosophy: Autobiographical Exercises* (Cambridge, MA: Harvard University Press, 1994), p. vii; *Little Did I Know: Excerpts from Memory* (Stanford, CA: Stanford University Press, 2010), 6.

Antonio Damasio, *The Feeling of What Happens: Body, Emotion and the Making of Consciousness* (London: Heinemann, 1999), 218–19.

Jerome S. Bruner, *Actual Minds, Possible Worlds* (Cambridge, MA: Harvard University Press, 1986), ch. 2.

Oliver Sacks, *The Man Who Mistook His Wife for a Hat* (London: Duckworth, 1985), 110.

Jerome Bruner, 'The Autobiographical Process', in Robert Folkenflik (ed.), *The Culture of Autobiography* (Stanford, CA: Stanford University Press, 1993), 38.

Daniel C. Dennett, *Times Literary Supplement*, September 16–22, 1988. Cited in Galen Strawson, *Real Materialism: And Other Essays* (Oxford: Clarendon Press, 1988), 196.

Charles Taylor, *Sources of the Self* (Cambridge, MA: Harvard University Press, 1989), 36; 111; 143; 185.

Paul Ricœur, 'Le soi et l'identité narrative', in Paul Ricœur, *Soi-même comme un autre* (Paris: Seuil, 1990), p. 187.

Taylor, *Sources*, 289.

Galen Strawson, 'Against Narrativity', *Ratio*, 17 (4 December 2004), 428–52. See also Strawson, 'The Unstoried Life', in Zachary Leader (ed.), *On Life-Writing* (Oxford: Oxford University Press, 2015), 284–301.

Derek Parfit, *Reasons and Persons* (Oxford: Clarendon Press, 1984), 281.

Jean-Paul Sartre, *La Nausée* (Paris: Gallimard, 1938), 64.

Michael Sheringham, *French Autobiography: Devices and Desires* (Oxford: Clarendon Press, 1993), 203.

Jean-Paul Sartre, *L'Être et le néant* (Paris: Gallimard, 1948), 651.

Simone de Beauvoir, *Tout compte fait* (Paris: Gallimard, 1972), 22.

André Gorz, *Le Traître* (Paris: Seuil, 2004), 64; 18.

Jean-Paul Sartre, *Les Mots* (Paris: Gallimard, 1963), 135; *Carnets de la drôle de guerre* (Paris: Gallimard, 1983).

Friedrich Nietzsche, *Ecce Homo: How to Become What You Are* (Oxford: Oxford University Press, 2007).

Friedrich Nietzsche, *Jenseits von Gut und Böse* (Munich: Wilhelm Goldmann, 1964), 10.

Søren Kierkegaard, *The Point of View for my Work as an Author* (Princeton University Press, 1998), 57.

Søren Kierkegaard, *Either/Or* (London: Penguin, 1992), 493.

David Hume, *The Life of David Hume, Esq. Written by Himself* (London: Printed for W. Strahan; and T. Cadell, in the Strand, 1777). Online at <https://ebooks.adelaide.edu.au/h/hume/david/life-of-david-hume-esq-written-by-himself/>. Accessed 16 December 2017.

Gillian Rose, *Love's Work* (London: Chatto and Windus, 1995).

Martin Warner, *The Aesthetics of Argument* (Oxford: Oxford University Press, 2016), 117.

Bertrand Russell, *Problems of Philosophy* (London: Williams and Norgate, 1912), ch. 15.

Bertrand Russell, *Autobiography* (London: George Allen and Unwin, 1967), vol. 1, 43; 152.

H. P. Rickman (ed.), *Wilhelm Dilthey: Selected Writings* (Cambridge: Cambridge University Press, 1976), 214.

Wilhelm Dilthey, *Selected Works*, ed. R. A. Makkreel and F. Rodi (Princeton, NJ: Princeton University Press, 1985–2010), vol. 3, 221; 216; 221.

Jacques Derrida, *De la grammatologie* (Paris: Minuit, 1967), 205.

Jacques Derrida, *L'Oreille de l'autre*, ed. Claude Lévesque and Christie V. McDonald (Montreal: VLB, 1982), 20; 25.

Jacques Derrida, '*Circonfession*', in Geoffrey Bennington and Jacques Derrida (eds) *Jacques Derrida* (Paris: Seuil, 1991).

Paul de Man, 'Autobiography as De-Facement', *Modern Language Notes*, 94(5) (December 1979), 919–30.

Maurice Halbwachs, *Les Cadres sociaux de la mémoire* (Paris: Albin Michel, 1994). *On Collective Memory*, ed. and tr. Lewis A. Coser (Chicago: University of Chicago Press, 1992).

Maurice Bloch, 'Time, Narratives and the Multiplicity of Representations of the Past', in Maurice Bloch, *How We Think They Think* (Boulder, CO: Westview Press, 1998), 100–13.

Maurice Bloch, 'The Blob', *Anthropology of this Century*, 1 (May 2011). <http://aotcpress.com/articles/blob/>. Accessed 16 December 2017.

Richard Terdiman, *Present Past: Modernity and the Memory Crisis* (Ithaca, NY and London: Cornell University Press, 1993), 240; 14. See also Anne Whitehead, *Memory* (Abingdon: Routledge, 2009).

See Denise Riley, *Time Lived, Without Its Flow* (London: Capsule Editions, 2012).

Michael Sheringham, 'Memory', in Margaretta Jolly (ed.), *Encyclopedia of Life Writing* (London: Fitzroy Dearborn, 2001), 597–8.

Chapter 4: Autobiography and psychoanalysis

W. H. Auden, 'In Memory of Sigmund Freud', *Amber Time* (New York: Random House, 1940).

J. M. Coetzee and Arabella Kurtz, *The Good Story: Exchanges on Truth, Fiction and Psychotherapy* (New York: Penguin, 2015), 3.

Lionel Trilling, *The Liberal Imagination: Essays on Literature and Society* (New York: Viking Press, 1950), 34–57.

Sigmund Freud, *The Interpretation of Dreams*, Standard Edition, vol. 4, tr. James Strachey (London: Hogarth Press, 1953), 105.

Sigmund Freud, *An Autobiographical Study*, Standard Edition, vol. 20.

The Complete Letters of Sigmund Freud to Wilhelm Fliess, 1887–1904, ed. Jeffrey Moussaieff Masson (Cambridge, MA and London: Harvard University Press, 1985), 264.

Sigmund Freud, 'Screen Memories', Standard Edition, vol. 3, 301–22, here 307; 309.

Sigmund Freud, *The Psychopathology of Everyday Life*, Standard Edition, vol. 6, 44; 47; 49.

Freud, 'Screen Memories', 322.

Sigmund Freud to Wilhelm Fliess, 272.

Sigmund Freud, *Leonardo da Vinci and a Memory of His Childhood*, Standard Edition, vol. 11.

The Freud/Jung Letters, ed. William McGuire (London: Penguin, 1991).

Erik Erikson, *Young Man Luther: A Study in Psychoanalysis and History* (New York and London: Norton, 1958); *Gandhi's Truth* (New York and London: Norton, 1969).

Arthur Koestler, *Arrow in the Blue* (London: Readers Union, 1954), 18.

J. B. Pontalis, *L'Amour des commencements* (Paris: Gallimard, 1986).

Michel Leiris, *L'Âge d'homme* (Paris: Gallimard, 1939), 218.

Charles Rycroft, 'On Autobiography', in Rycroft, *Psychoanalysis and Beyond* (London: Chatto and Windus, 1985), 192.

Katherine Mansfield, *Notebooks*, 29 April 1920, ed. Margaret Scott (Minneapolis: University of Minnesota Press, 2002).

Carl Jung, *Memories, Dreams, Reflections* (London and Glasgow: Collins Fontana, 1967), 185.

Freud, *The Interpretation of Dreams*, Standard Edition, vol. 5, 454.

Jung, *Memories*, 184–5; 225; 219; 222.

Edwin Muir, *An Autobiography* (London: Hogarth Press, 1987), 114; 157; 164; 14; 54.

H.D., *Tribute to Freud* (Manchester: Carcanet, 1985), 41.

Adrian Stokes, *Inside Out*, in *The Critical Writings of Adrian Stokes, Vol. II*, ed. Lawrence Gowing (London: Thames and Hudson, 1978), 141; 158; *Smooth and Rough*.

Richard Wollheim, *Germs: A Memoir of Childhood* (Baltimore and London: Waywiser Press, 2004).

Richard Wollheim, 'On Persons and their Lives', in A. O. Rorty (ed.), *Explaining Emotions* (Berkeley: University of California Press, 1980), 315.

Ronald Fraser, *A Search for the Past* (London: Verso, 1984).

Marie Cardinal, *The Words to Say it* (London: Pan, 1984), 53.

Bruno Bettelheim, 'Afterword', in Cardinal, *The Words to Say it*, 218.

Adam Gopnik, 'Man Goes to See a Doctor', in Adam Gopnik, *Through the Children's Gate* (London: Quercus, 2006), 37–55.

Dan Gunn, *Wool-Gathering or How I Ended Analysis* (Hove: Brunner-Routledge, 2002), 38.

Chapter 5: Family histories and the autobiography of childhood

Jean-Paul Sartre, *Les Mots* (Paris: Gallimard, 1963), 70; 18; 28.

Philippe Ariès, *Centuries of Childhood* (London: Jonathan Cape, 1962), 216.

Edward Gibbon, *Memoirs of My Life*, ed. Betty Radice (London: Penguin, 1984), 41; 60; 154.

John Stuart Mill, *An Autobiography*, *Collected Works*, ed. John M. Robson and Jack Stillinger (Indianapolis: Liberty Fund, 1992), vol. 1, 5; 9; 55; 143; 145; 151.

Jean-François Marmontel, *Mémoires d'un père* (London: Peltier, 1805).

Edmund Gosse, *Father and Son* (London: Penguin, 1989), 35; 235.

Augustine, *Confessions*, 168.

J. R. Ackerley, *My Father and Myself* (London: Bodley Head, 1968).

Blake Morrison, *And When Did You Last See Your Father?* (London: Granta Books, 1993), 169.

John Burnside, *A Lie About My Father* (London: Jonathan Cape, 2006), 45; 17–18.

Paul Auster, *The Invention of Solitude* (New York: Penguin, 1982), 14.

Andrew O'Hagan, 'Guilt: A Memoir', *London Review of Books*, 31(21) (5 November 2009), 42–3. <https://www.lrb.co.uk/v31/n21/andrew-ohagan/guilt>. Accessed 16 December 2017.

Dave Pelzer, *A Child Called 'It'* (London: Orion, 2000).

Frank McCourt, *Angela's Ashes* (London: Harper, 1996), 1.

Andrea Ashworth, *Once in a House on Fire* (London: Picador, 1998).

Jeanette Winterson, *Oranges Are Not the Only Fruit* (London: Pandora Press, 1985).

Jeanette Winterson, *Why Be Happy When You Could Be Normal?* (London: Jonathan Cape, 2011), 6; 223; 5.

Hilary Mantel, *Giving up the Ghost* (London: Fourth Estate, 2003), 217.

Mary McCarthy, *Memories of a Catholic Girlhood* (San Diego, New York and London: Harcourt, 1957).

Paul Thompson, *The Voice of the Past: Oral History*, 4th edition (Oxford: Oxford University Press, 2017).

Carolyn Steedman, *Landscape for a Good Woman* (London: Virago, 1986), 5; 22.

Lorna Sage, *Bad Blood: A Memoir* (London: Fourth Estate, 2000), 3; 15.

Simone de Beauvoir, *Mémoires d'une jeune fille rangée* (Paris: Gallimard, 1958), 359.

Sara Suleri, *Meatless Days: A Memoir* (London: William Collins, 1989), 177; 77; 92.

Gloria Anzaldúa, *Borderlands/La Frontera* (San Francisco: Aunt Lute Books, 1987).

Assia Djebar, *Fantasia: An Algerian Cavalcade* (London: Heinemann, 1993).

Maxine Hong Kingston, *The Woman Warrior: Memoirs of a Girlhood Among Ghosts* (New York: Vintage, 1989), 291.

Gibbon, *Memoirs of My Life*, 60; 61.

Chapter 6: Public selves

Andrew Carnegie, *Autobiography of Andrew Carnegie* (London: Constable, 1920), 48.

Barack Obama, *Dreams From My Father* (Edinburgh: Canongate, 2007), xvii; 25–6; xvi.

Arthur Koestler, *Arrow in the Blue* (London: Readers Union, 1954), 19; *The Invisible Writing* (London: Collins, 1954).

Nelson Mandela, *Long Walk to Freedom* (New York: Little Brown, 1994), 477.

Emma Goldman, *Living My Life* (New York: Knopf, 1931), 616.

Obama, *Dreams*, xv.

Günter Grass, *Beim Häuten der Zwiebel* (Göttingen: Steidl, 2006).

Edward Said, *Out of Place* (London: Granta, 1999), 222; 'No Reconciliation Allowed', in André Aciman (ed.), *Letters of Transit* (New York: The New Press, 1999), 112.

Malcolm X, with the assistance of Alex Haley, *The Autobiography of Malcolm X* (London: Penguin, 2007), 8; 78.

Tony Blair, *A Journey* (New York: Random House, 2010), xlvii.

Andrew O'Hagan, 'Ghosting', *London Review of Books*, 36(5) (6 March 2014), 5–26.

Decca Aitkenhead, 'How I Got Rio to Relive the Hardest Days of His Life', *The Guardian* (31 October 2017), section g2, 14–15.

Dorothy Parker, 'The Autobiography of Any Movie Actress', *Vanity Fair* (September 1919).

Chapter 7: Self-portraiture, photography, and performance

Michel Beaujour, *Miroirs d'encre* (Paris: Seuil, 1980), 10.

James Hall, *The Self-Portrait: A Cultural History* (London: Thames & Hudson, 2014), 19.

Julian Bell, *500 Self-Portraits* (London: Phaidon, 2000), 5.

Rainer Maria Rilke, *Notebooks of Malte Laurids Brigge* (New York: Norton, 1949), 14–15.

Robert Folkenflik, 'The Self as Other', in Robert Folkenflik (ed.), *The Culture of Autobiography* (Stanford, CA: Stanford University Press, 1993), 234. The psychoanalytic theorist and practitioner Jacques Lacan conceived the 'mirror stage' as the moment when an infant forms a (partly illusory) image of itself.

W. H. Auden, 'The Dyer's Hand' (London: Faber, 1963), 96.

Michel de Montaigne, *Essais* (Paris: PUF, 1924).

Laura Cumming, *A Face to the World: On Self-Portraits* (London: Harper Press, 2009), 84; 88.

Jean-Jacques Rousseau, 'Préambule du manuscrit de Neuchâtel'. <https://www.autopacte.org/Rousseau-pr%E9ambule-Neuch%E2tel.html>. Accessed 16 December 2017.

Benvenuto Cellini, *Autobiography*, tr. George Bull (Harmondsworth: Penguin, 1956), 15; 345–7.

Vincent van Gogh, *Dear Theo: The Autobiography of Vincent Van Gogh*, ed. Irving and Jean Stone (New York: Penguin, 1969), Preface, viii.

Benjamin Robert Haydon, *Life of Haydon from His Autobiography and Journals* (London: Longman, 1853).

William Holman Hunt, *Pre-Raphaelitism and the Pre-Raphaelite Brotherhood* (London: Macmillan, 1905).

John Ruskin, *Praeterita* (Oxford: Oxford University Press, 1978), 255.

Michael Baxendall, *Episodes: A Memory Book* (London: Frances Lincoln, 2010), 72.

Walter Pater, 'The Child in the House' (1878), reprinted in Walter Pater, *Miscellaneous Essays* (Teddington: Echo, 2006), 79.

Baxendall, *Episodes*, 55.

J. B. Pontalis, *L'Amour des commencements* (Paris: Gallimard, 1986).

Nicéphore Niépce produced the first photograph in 1826.

Roland Barthes, *Roland Barthes by Roland Barthes* (Paris: Points, 2015).

Michael Ignatieff, *Russian Album*, 2nd edition (New York: Picador, 1997), 4–7.

Baxendall, *Episodes*, 44.

Freud, 'Screen Memories', Standard Edition, vol. 3 (London: Hogarth Press, 1953), 322.

Siegfried Kracauer, 'Photography', tr. Thomas Y. Levin, *Critical Inquiry*, 19(3) (Spring 1993), 421–36.

Vladimir Nabokov, *Speak, Memory: An Autobiography Revisited* (Harmondsworth: Penguin, 1966), 22–3; 18; 120; 130.

Susan Sontag, *On Photography* (London: Penguin, 1997), 15.

Roland Barthes, *La Chambre claire* (Paris: Gallimard, 1980), 121; 115.

Annette Kuhn, *Family Secrets* (London: Verso, 1995), 6; 40; 93; 3.

J. R. Ackerley, *My Father and Myself* (London: Bodley Head, 1968), 199.

Paul Auster, *The Invention of Solitude* (New York: Penguin, 1988), 33; 36.

Susan Faludi, *In the Darkroom* (London: Collins, 2016), 34.

Michael Ondaatje, *Running in the Family* (London: Gollancz, 1983).

Orhan Pamuk, *Istanbul: Memories and the City*, tr. Maureen Freely (London: Faber, 2005), 38; 33.

André Breton, *Nadja* (Paris: NRF, 1928).

Jill Walker Rettberg, *Seeing Ourselves Through Technology* (London: Palgrave, 2014), 88. See also Katie Warfield, 'Digital Subjectivities and Selfies: The Model, the Self-Conscious Thespian, and the #realme', *International Journal of the Image*, 6(2) (June 2015), 1–16.

Chapter 8: Autobiographies, autobiographical novels, and autofictions

Max Saunders, *Self Impression* (Oxford: Oxford University Press, 2010), 165–79.

Stephen Reynolds, 'Autobiografiction', *Speaker* 15:66 (1906).

Henri Bergson, *Mélanges*, ed. André Robinet (Paris: Presses Universitaires de France, 1972), 1055.

Katherine Mansfield, *The Katherine Mansfield Notebooks*, ed. Margaret Scott (Canterbury, New Zealand: Lincoln University Press, 2002), vol. 2, 204.

T. S. Eliot, 'Tradition and the Individual Talent', in T. S. Eliot, *Selected Prose* (Harmondsworth: Penguin, 1953), 26; 28.

D. H. Lawrence, 'Mushrooms', cited in John Worthen (ed.), *D. H. Lawrence: The Early Years 1885–1912* (Cambridge: Cambridge University Press, 1991), vii.

James T. Boulton and Margaret H. Boulton (eds), *The Letters of D. H. Lawrence* (Cambridge: Cambridge University Press, 1991), 465.

Dorothy Richardson, 'Data for a Spanish Publisher', in Richardson, *Journey to Paradise*, ed. Trudi Tate (London: Virago, 1989), 112.

The Letters of Virginia Woolf, vol. 6, 1936–41 (Harmondsworth: Penguin, 1980), 453.

Paul Ricœur, *Time and Narrative*, vol. 3, tr. Kathleen Blamey and David Pellauer (Chicago: University of Chicago Press, 1988), 246.

V. S. Naipaul, *Finding the Centre* (Harmondsworth: Penguin, 1985), 87.

Serge Doubrovsky, *Fils* (Paris: Grasset, 1977).

Philippe Lejeune, *Moi aussi* (Paris: Seuil, 1986), 24; 64.

Coster, cited by Lejeune, *Moi aussi*, 54.

Jesse Barron, 'Completely Without Dignity: An Interview with Karl Ove Knausgaard', *Paris Review* (26 December 2013). <https://www.theparisreview.org/blog/2013/12/26/completely-without-dignity-an-interview-with-karl-ove-knausgaard/>. Accessed 16 December 2017.

Joshua Rothman, 'Knausgaard's Selflessness', *New Yorker* (20 April 2016). <https://www.newyorker.com/books/page-turner/knausgaards-selflessness>. Accessed 16 December 2017.

Chris Kraus, *I Love Dick* (Los Angeles: Semiotext(e), 1997).

Rachel Cooke, 'Novelist Chris Kraus: "Who Hasn't Had an Affair?"', *The Guardian* (30 April 2017). <https://www.theguardian.com/books/2017/apr/30/chris-kraus-ive-never-had-much-talent-for-making-things-up-i-love-dick-interview>. Accessed 16 December 2017.

Elle Hunt, 'Chris Kraus: I Love Dick Was Written "In a Delirium"', *The Guardian* (20 May 2017). <https://www.theguardian.com/books/2017/may/30/chris-kraus-i-love-dick-was-written-in-a-delirium>. Accessed 16 December 2017.

Sheila Heti, *How Should a Person Be?* (Toronto: House of Anansi Press, 2010).

Thessaly La Force, 'Sheila Heti on How Should a Person Be?', *Paris Review* (18 June 2012). <https://www.theparisreview.org/blog/2012/06/18/sheila-heti-on-how-should-a-person-be/>. Accessed 16 December 2017.

James Wood, 'My Brilliant Friend', *New Yorker* (19 December 2013). <https://www.newyorker.com/books/page-turner/favorite-books-of-2013>. Accessed 16 December 2017.

Liz Jobey, 'Women of 2015: Elena Ferrante', *Financial Times* (11 December 2015). <https://www.believermag.com/issues/200711/?read=interview_hickey>. Accessed 16 December 2017.

Nicole Krauss, *Forest Dark* (New York: HarperCollins 2017).

Erica Wagner, 'Nicole Krauss: "The Self is More or Less an Invention from Beginning to End"', *The Guardian* (20 August 2017). <https://www.theguardian.com/books/2017/aug/20/nicole-krauss-forest-dark-self-israel-kafka-interview>. Accessed 16 December 2017.

Mark Twain, Letter to William D. Howells, 14 March 1904. <http://www.gutenberg.org/files/3197/3197-h/3197-h.htm#link2H_4_0004>. Accessed 16 December 2017.

Further reading

Linda Anderson, *Autobiography* (London: Routledge, 2001).

Maria DiBattista and Emily O. Wittman (eds), *The Cambridge Companion to Autobiography* (Cambridge: Cambridge University Press, 2014).

Robert Folkenflik (ed.), *The Culture of Autobiography* (Stanford, CA: Stanford University Press, 1993).

Margaretta Jolly (ed.), *Encyclopedia of Life Writing*, 2 vols (London: Fitzroy Dearborn, 2001).

Zachary Leader (ed.), *On Life-Writing* (Oxford: Oxford University Press, 2015).

Philippe Lejeune, *On Autobiography*, tr. Katherine Leary (Minneapolis: University of Minnesota Press, 1989).

Laura Marcus, *Auto/biographical Discourses: Theory, Criticism, Practice* (Manchester: Manchester University Press, 1994).

James Olney (ed.), *On Autobiography* (Princeton, NJ: Princeton University Press, 1980).

Linda Haverty Rugg, *Picturing Ourselves: Photography and Autobiography* (Chicago: University of Chicago Press, 1997).

Max Saunders, *Self Impression: Life-Writing, Autobiografiction, and the Forms of Modern Literature* (Oxford: Oxford University Press, 2010).

Michael Sheringham, *French Autobiography: Devices and Desires* (Oxford: Clarendon Press, 1993).

Adam Smyth (ed.), *A History of English Autobiography* (Cambridge: Cambridge University Press, 2016).

Liz Stanley, *The Auto/biographical I* (Manchester: Manchester University Press, 1992).

Paul Thompson, *The Voice of the Past: Oral History*, 4th edition (Oxford: Oxford University Press, 2017).

Julia Watson and Sidonie Smith, *Reading Autobiography: A Guide for Interpreting Life Narratives*, 2nd edition (Minneapolis: University of Minnesota Press, 2010).

Alex Zwerdling, *The Rise of the Memoir* (Oxford: Oxford University Press, 2017).

Publisher's acknowledgements

We are grateful for permission to include the following copyright material in this book.

forty-two (42) words from CONFESSIONS by Saint Augustine, translated with an introduction by R. S. Pine-Coffin (Penguin Classics, 1961). Copyright © R. S. Pine-Coffin, 1961.

twenty-seven (27) words from EITHER/OR: A FRAGMENT OF LIFE Søren Kierkegaard, edited by Victor Eremita, abridged, translated and with an introduction and notes by Alastair Hannay (Penguin Classics, 1992). Copyright © Alastair Hannay, 1992.

fifty-four (54) words from AUTOBIOGRAPHY by Benvenuto Cellini, translated with an introduction by George Bull (Penguin Books, 1956). Copyright © George Bull, 1956.

Extracts from The Standard Edition of the Complete Psychological Works of Sigmund Freud, vol. III, translated and edited by James Strachey by Sigmund Freud published by Hogarth Press. Reproduced by permission of The Random House Group Ltd ©

Extract from M.K. Gandhi, An Autobiography, tr. Mahadev Desai, Penguin, London, 2001. Reproduced by permission of Navajivan Trust ©

The publisher and author have made every effort to trace and contact all copyright holders before publication. If notified, the publisher will be pleased to rectify any errors or omissions at the earliest opportunity.

Index

BIOGRAPHY
A Very Short Introduction
Hermione Lee

Biography is one of the most popular, best-selling, and widely-read of literary genres. But why do certain people and historical events arouse so much interest? How can biographies be compared with history and works of fiction? Does a biography need to be true? Is it acceptable to omit or conceal things? Does the biographer need to personally know the subject? Must a biographer be subjective? In this *Very Short Introduction* Hermione Lee considers the cultural and historical background of different types of biographies, looking at the factors that affect biographers and whether there are different strategies, ethics, and principles required for writing about one person compared to another. She also considers contemporary biographical publications and considers what kind of 'lives' are the most popular and in demand.

'It would be hard to think of anyone better to provide a crisp contribution to OUP's Very Short Introductions.'

Kathryn Hughes, The Guardian

www.oup.com/vsi

ENGLISH LITERATURE

A Very Short Introduction

Jonathan Bate

Sweeping across two millennia and every literary genre, acclaimed scholar and biographer Jonathan Bate provides a dazzling introduction to English Literature. The focus is wide, shifting from the birth of the novel and the brilliance of English comedy to the deep Englishness of landscape poetry and the ethnic diversity of Britain's Nobel literature laureates. It goes on to provide a more in-depth analysis, with close readings from an extraordinary scene in King Lear to a war poem by Carol Ann Duffy, and a series of striking examples of how literary texts change as they are transmitted from writer to reader.

{No reviews}

www.oup.com/vsi

SOCIAL MEDIA
Very Short Introduction

Join our community

www.oup.com/vsi

- Join us online at the official Very Short Introductions **Facebook** page.
- Access the thoughts and musings of our authors with our online **blog**.
- Sign up for our monthly **e-newsletter** to receive information on all new titles publishing that month.
- Browse the full range of Very Short Introductions online.
- Read **extracts** from the Introductions for free.
- If you are a teacher or lecturer you can order inspection copies quickly and simply via our website.